PRAISE FOR THE UNLEASHED CHURCH

"This book is exactly what the church needs! It clarifies the often confusing subject of spiritual gifts in a way that is helpful, practical and biblical. Your life will benefit, your church will benefit, and the surrounding world will benefit from this book. I urge you to read it and put it into practice in your own life. You will find a renewed sense of purpose in your ministry and joy in your Christian service. Thank you Rob Pochek!"

Dr. Doug Munton
Senior Pastor
First Baptist Church, O'Fallon, IL

"Rob Pochek has served the church well by calling the church to rescue spiritual gifts from psychometric testers developing formulas in office parks. Christ has already provided a means for testing spiritual gifts and it is not accomplished alone at a desk with a scantron sheet. Christ calls us to passionately serve the body of Christ laboring with and listening to other Christians. While serving in the church, hidden gifts are often brought to light and the community of faith provides a needed corrective or affirmation of what we supposed to be our gifting."

David E. Prince, Ph.D.
Pastor of Preaching and Vision,
Ashland Ave Baptist Church, Lexington, KY
Assistant Prof of Preaching,
The Southern Baptist Theological Seminary,
Louisville, KY

"A fresh and relevant examination of spiritual giftedness and their consequent use for Kingdom work in the 21st century."

Rev. Greg L. Carr
Senior Associate Pastor
Raleigh Road Baptist Church, Wilson, NC

The Unleashed Church

A New Understanding of Spiritual Gifts to Move People from
Attenders to Participants

© 2014 by Rob Pochek

Published by Rainer Publishing
www.rainerpublishing.com

ISBN 978-0692322383

Scripture quotations are from The Holy Bible, English
Standard Version® (ESV®), copyright © 2001 by Crossway, a
publishing ministry of Good News Publishers. Used by
permission. All rights reserved.

Printed in the United States of America

CONTENTS

ACKNOWLEDGEMENTS

Any time a person puts their words in print for all to see (and evaluate) it is a daunting and frightening thing. In addition to the Lord Jesus Christ, I am indebted to a number of people whose encouragement led to the work you have in your hands.

I am thankful first and foremost to my parents. God graciously drew them to faith in 1977. From the earliest days of their walk with God they were always "Berean" in their approach to biblical, spiritual, and theological issues. They taught my two sisters (Jennifer and Shelly) and me that our views should be shaped first and finally by what the Bible says. It was that encouragement that led me to tackle the accepted practice of using spiritual gift inventories to determine where one should serve in my Ph.D. dissertation.

I am thankful for the good folks at Rainer Publishing for seeing value in making a fairly technical dissertation available in a much more reader friendly form. I am hopeful that the work will not disappoint them.

I am indebted to my good friend Pastor Greg Carr of his initial editing of this work. He has a penchant for finding grammatical and spelling errors and inconsistencies. I am happy to acknowledge I provided many for him to happily point out to me.

I am also thankful for Charles Gooch, Jr.'s reading and comments on the book. Charles is a member of the church I serve and he went above and beyond in helping craft this work into what it is today.

Finally, I am thankful to my wife Susy and my children, David and Jessica. They endured many days and nights of an absentee husband and father while I worked on the dissertation phase of this material. Now that it is in this form, I hope they will take some measure of pride in the role they played in making it a reality.

For better or worse, this book is the culmination of many years of thinking about the issue of spiritual gifts. If there is anything of redeeming value, it is by God's grace alone. For those areas that are not as redeeming, I take sole responsibility.

INTRODUCTION

Eight letters. It took only eight letters to help transform a growing Portland area shoe company into the world's largest sporting goods maker. Only eight letters, yet the impact of those eight letters on the athletic shoe market is undeniable. What words did those eight letters form? Just Do It!

That simple slogan was coined by advertising executive Dan Wieden for his company's most famous client, Nike.[1] Unfortunately for Wieden, all of the success that followed his eight letter campaign almost never happened. Nike executives initially were lukewarm to his idea. After all, their previous ad tagline – "there is no finish line" – had been more obviously sport specific. However, because they were losing the shoe battle to Reebok, they were open to giving it a try. Or, I guess you could say, they decided to . . . Just Do It!

Nearly twenty-five years later and those eight letters are now ensconced in popular culture – not only in the United States, but also around the world. In fact, the 1988 "Just Do It" Nike ad campaign was chosen by *Advertising Age* as one of the top five ad slogans of the 20th century and enshrined in the Smithsonian Institution. What helped to push the ad campaign from successful shoe sales into the realm of iconic culture phrase, however, was that it had application far beyond the scope of sports. In fact, Nike reports that people have written them expressing gratitude for the tagline's influence in their lives. Some of those people had walked away from abusive husbands or had attempted heroic feats as a result of the eight letter directive to Just Do It.

The ad campaign was hugely successful for a number of reasons. Practically, it was a tag line that could be used with any number of sports. In fact, in 2007 a Just Do It commercial featured NBA players, Kenyan runners, mixed martial artists, weightlifters, and professional tennis players, among others. The ad campaign was not successful solely because of the work of advertisers. The fact is that the ad campaign is a call to action that played into our competitive nature. More than that, it played into one of the deepest failings of the fallen human heart – the tendency toward self-reliance. Just Do It.

"Just Do It" and the Church

Since the early 1970s a significant number of churches in the United States have increasingly regarded a conscious understanding of spiritual gifts and the utilization of those gifts in the life of the church as important for individual followers of Christ. Over the past thirty-five years or so, an increasingly large amount of material on the subject of spiritual gifts has been produced. C. Peter Wagner, a prolific writer on the subject of spiritual gifts, is a strong advocate for the use of spiritual gifts in the life of the church. Wagner contends that there is no "dimension of the Christian life that more effectively joins the teachings of Scripture with the day-to-day activities of the people of God than spiritual gifts."[2] Thom Rainer is a scholar, researcher, and prolific writer in his own right. He suggests that churches will grow as Christians discover their spiritual gifts and then use those gifts to build up the body of Christ.[3]

The effort of local churches to help people discover their spiritual gifts has the goal of helping people to get engaged in the ministry of the local church. This effort has created a plethora of material, including books, seminars, and spiritual gift inventories (both paper based and online). Of these resources, the "spiritual gift inventory" has become a frequently used method by which churches aim to help believers discover their spiritual gifts. Yet is the use of a spiritual gift identification instrument the best way for people to find their place of joyful service within the church? Or, could the church learn something from the good folks at Nike?

It goes without saying that there is a lot of debate among scholars, pastors and lay people about the nature and purpose of spiritual gifts. Most of these debates pertain to the nature of certain gifts (i.e. tongues, healing, etc.) and whether those gifts are still active today. Although there is debate about some gifts, the conventional view seems to be that spiritual gifts are divine abilities given to believers by the Holy Spirit at conversion. Yet there is terribly little in the Scripture to support this view. Indeed, it is my contention that the emphasis on divine enablement has led to an unfortunate and fundamental misunderstanding of the best way to "discover" spiritual gifts, namely the use of spiritual gift inventories.

A Little Background

Three threads have been woven together in my life to create an interest in studying spiritual gifts and spiritual gift inventories: my personal journey of faith in Christ; my academic course of study; and my experience as a pastor in the local church. Each of these threads has served to strengthen my resolve to better understand how to help believers joyfully serve in the church of Jesus Christ, in the power of the Holy Spirit, to the glory of God.

My interest in spiritual gift inventories began shortly after becoming a follower of Christ at 11 years of age. A few years later, our pastor led our church to utilize a spiritual gift inventory to help people find their most effective place of ministry within the church. Even though I was only a teenage believer, I was encouraged to complete the spiritual gift inventory. Yet even as a teen, I had questions about where the instrument came from, who developed it, and whether or not it was a "biblical" tool. Indeed, I vividly remember wondering "what would Paul think of this?"

During my college and seminary years I recall hearing professors suggest that spiritual gift inventories were not very accurate and probably not the best method of determining spiritual gifts. Yet no one seemed to offer a better strategy. And worse, no one seemed to have any definitive "proof" that spiritual gift inventories were not very reliable. So, when I had to select a topic to research for my Ph.D. dissertation at The Southern Baptist Theological Seminary, the choice was easy: spiritual gift inventories.[4]

My desire, however, was never to create a research document that remained solely in the halls of academia. My desire has always been to equip God's people to better and more effectively serve him. Thus, I have sought to take academic research and present it to God's people in order to help us all serve Christ more faithfully.

An Overview of S.U.RV.E.

The *S.U.RV.E.* strategy for the unleashed church is derived from the research and conclusions contained in my Ph.D. dissertation. My goal here is to help you answer the question: What is the best way to find my place of joyful service in the church? Needless to say, I do not believe it is taking a spiritual gift inventory! Nor do I desire to provide yet another program that promises to answer all your questions. Rather, the four components of *S.U.RV.E.* comprise an ongoing process. Rather than the typical "do these four things" approach so popular in self-help writing, the four components of *S.U.RV.E.* are intended to be more like the final instruction on your shampoo bottle . . .Wash, rinse, repeat! In other words, these four components should be incorporated into your life (and the life of your church) and continually revisited as you seek to honor God with your gifts and talents.

As you might have guessed, *S.U.RV.E.* is an acrostic for the unleashed church with each letter representing another component of the process:

S – Seek God's Face in Prayer
U – Understand Spiritual Gifts
R V – Regularly Volunteer
E – Evaluate for Effectiveness

This may sound like a fairly straight-forward process. But for many Christ followers, figuring out how to serve God is anything but straight-forward. We are inundated with ideas about how to discover spiritual gifts, about not relying on natural talents, hearing a call from God to serve in a given area, and the like. The goal of *S.U.RV.E.* is to remove much of the anxiety and frustration of trying to figure out where to serve and to free Christ followers to serve faithfully and fruitfully.

The first chapter, "Seek God's Face in Prayer," is the foundation of the *S.U.RV.E.* process. When confronted with large crowds of people who needed to be ministered to, Jesus told his followers to "ask the Lord of the harvest, therefore, to send out workers into his harvest field." (Mt 9:38). Prayer is crucial if God's people are going to discover where they would serve most effectively. Why? Because God knows how he has made you and where you best fit in the ministry of the church. Seeking his face is essential. Yet it is amazing how many believers would rather fill out a quick online survey to determine their spiritual gift rather than spend that same amount of time in prayer asking God for direction and guidance.

The second and third chapters are entitled "Understand Spiritual Gifts." Since the understanding of spiritual gifts proposed here is a bit different than the conventional view, this component of *S.U.RV.E.* is broken into two sections.

Chapter two focuses on critiquing the conventional view of spiritual gifts in light of the New Testament teaching about spiritual gifts. By "conventional view" I mean the definition of spiritual gifts as "divine abilities" that are granted at conversion and that are found in 1 Corinthians 12, Romans 12, and Ephesians 4. It is this view that has led to a hyper-personalization of spiritual gifts and the proliferation of instruments that purport to reveal your gifts by answering a handful of questions.

Chapter three moves toward the practical application of the New Testament view described in chapter two by suggesting a different approach to understanding spiritual gifts. Specifically, the radically biblical idea that God often gifts, equips and calls people in keeping with their "birth" gifts is proposed and defended. It is this component of *S.U.RV.E.* that challenges believers to reflect on their skills, talents, and passions in assessing where God would have them serve. So many people do not serve in the local church because of the misconception that they cannot "do anything." Yet these same people spent their lives utilizing tremendous skills in the workplace and exercising tremendous talent and passion pursuing their hobbies. The *S.U.RV.E.* process encourages believers to bring these areas of their life together in order to advance God's kingdom.

The fourth chapter, "Regularly Volunteer" intends to encourage believers to begin serving wherever the opportunities present themselves. With the freedom discovered in the preceding chapters, most believers will realize that God has equipped them to be a blessing in the church. And that newfound reality will enable them to serve more readily. In addition, suggestions are provided for how to approach church leaders for guidance in where your skills are most needed.

The fifth chapter, "Evaluate for Effectiveness" is a reminder that, occasionally, there is a gap between our understandings of where God would have us serving and where our skills, talents and passion would be most effective. Evaluation is a beneficial component of the *S.U.RV.E.* process for both the church and the believer. Few people want to continue serving in areas they are ineffective. And few churches want people serving in areas where they are ineffective. Evaluation is the key to helping assess whether the believer's skills, talents and passion and the church's needs have aligned. The role of evaluation should be carried out by church leadership, or those designated by church leadership, in consultation with the believer. The intent is for evaluation to be a positive experience for all involved.

Finally, let me say this: I love the local church. I believe in the local church. Quite literally, the hope of the world – the gospel – has been entrusted to the local church. The local church is the best place in which every believer can be a part of advancing the gospel. Yet in so many ways, we have made it overly complicated for believers to serve faithfully in the church. It is my desire that the *S.U.RV.E.* strategy will be a blessing to you as you seek to discover your place of joyful service in the church. It is my prayer that this book will start you on a never-ending journey of selfless, Christ-honoring service in the local church.

CHAPTER ONE

Seek God's Face in Prayer

I am a fan of action movies; especially military-based action movies. Whether they are set in modern times (i.e. *Lone Survivor*), the recent past (i.e. *Saving Private Ryan*) or the distant past (i.e. *Braveheart*) these movies teach lessons that are useful to leaders in organizations of any kind. One such movie is *Crimson Tide,* a 1995 film starring Gene Hackman and Denzel Washington. The film was set aboard a U.S. Navy nuclear submarine, the USS *Alabama* – thus the name Crimson Tide – during a time of political unrest in post-Soviet Russia, caused by military units loyal to Vladimir Radchenko, an ultranationalist. Radchenko's followers have taken control of a nuclear missile installation and are threatening nuclear war if either the American or Russian governments attempt to confront him.

The *Alabama* is assigned a patrol mission, to be available to launch its missiles in a preemptive strike if Radchenko attempts to fuel his missiles. Captain Frank Ramsey (Hackman) is the commanding officer of the sub, and one of the few commanders left in the U.S. Navy with any combat experience. He chooses as his new executive officer (XO) Lieutenant Commander Ron Hunter (Washington), who has an extensive education in military history and tactics, but no combat experience.

During their initial days at sea, tensions between Ramsey and Hunter become apparent due to a clash of personalities. Hunter takes a more analytical, cautious approach to leadership, as opposed to Ramsey's more impulsive and intuitive approach. The *Alabama* eventually receives an Emergency Action Message, ordering the launch of ten of its missiles against the Russian nuclear installation, based on satellite information that the Russians' missiles are being fueled. Before the *Alabama* can launch, a second message arrives but is cut off by the attack of a Russian submarine loyal to Radchenko. The radio is damaged in the attack and is unable to decode the second message. With the last confirmed order being to launch, Captain Ramsey decides to proceed. Hunter refuses to concur as is procedurally required, because he believes the partial second message may be a retraction. As you can imagine, the film's intensity builds as Captain Ramsey and Hunter struggle for control of the ship and its nuclear arsenal.

Beneath all the political intrigue, personality clashes, and tension in this Hollywood blockbuster is a simple problem: the radio is broken. Simply put, they have a communication problem. The sailors on the *Alabama* do not know what to do next because they cannot communicate with their superiors. The lack of communication sends the crew into such disarray that they are literally fighting each other.

The Priority of Prayer

Consider this: God has created us to play a role in the grand drama of redemption. And when we are not engaged in what he created us for, we end up taking out our frustration on those around us. The tension on the bridge of the *Alabama* is a pretty good picture of a fair number of churches. When believers are unclear of their instructions, they turn on each other. If we are to avoid the kind of drama that does a good job selling movie tickets (but destroys churches), we need to communicate with the God of heaven to get clear instructions.

Ken Berding notes that a person wondering where they should serve "need ask only a single question–a question asked repeatedly throughout the history of Christianity: 'Lord, where do you want me to serve?'"[5] In other words, PRAY! Prayer is critical because the most effective method in determining where God would have us to serve is to know God. On this point, Henry and Mel Blackaby comment, "Here again we must emphasize this truth: *The relationship is the key.* You must know Christ well enough that you already know your answer before He tells you the assignment. The answer must be 'Yes, Lord.' You'll need to trust that God knows what He's doing. We must never look first at ourselves, our abilities, and our desires to determine whether we will obey or not (italics his)."[6]

It is through prayer that we come to know the heart of the Father for those whose hearts are far from Him. It is through prayer that His desire for how we can make a difference in the lives of those apart from him becomes clear. In short, it is through prayer that the needs of the world around us and the resources the Father has entrusted to us come together. And it is through prayer that our hearts are gently bent by the Holy Spirit toward obedience.

Placing a priority on prayer is crucial for the individual Christian and for those in church leadership. As both seek God's face, clarity as to whom God has set apart for various ministry assignments and tasks will become clear. Prayer will often require patience, but it is worth the wait. Unfortunately, those of us heavily influenced by Western culture tend to be concerned with timeliness, effectiveness and efficiency. And, let's be honest, prayer does not always seem very efficient. We want to do "something."

While we are waiting on the Lord, it can be very tempting to take one of those handy-dandy spiritual gift inventories. But is that best? Ken Hemphill, an expert in the area of spiritual gifts does not think so. Indeed, Hemphill advocates prayer as a priority and laments that he is "saddened to discover that many Christians would rather spend thirty minutes filling out a gift inventory than thirty minutes talking with their Father about their giftedness."[7] I have served in ministry for nearly twenty years, and have earned a graduate degree specializing in church growth methods, and there is little doubt that Hemphill is right. Our approach tends to be 180 degrees opposite of what Jesus advocated for his first followers.

Why Prayer?

There are a number of reasons why we should begin with prayer. The most important (and obvious) is that in prayer we are not only speaking to God, but we are also open to Him speaking to us. How does God speak to us in prayer? There are a number of ways the Bible describes God leading His people in prayer, not the least of which is putting something in our heart (or mind). In the book of Nehemiah, the prophet describes God putting something in his heart (Neh 2:12, see also Neh 7:5). In Nehemiah 2:12 he clarifies that it was God who put in his heart the plan to rebuild the walls of Jerusalem. When did God do that? We can surmise from Nehemiah 1:4 that it was during Nehemiah's extended period of mourning, fasting, and prayer. It was then that the needs of his former hometown and the resources the Father had entrusted to him came together. Later in Nehemiah 7:5 a similar thing happens. This time, in response to the lack of people residing in the city, Nehemiah gathers the people together. According to Nehemiah he engaged in this particular course of action because "my God put it in my heart."

Paul echoes a similar sentiment in Acts 20:22 when he is bidding farewell to the elders at Ephesus. He shares with them that he must go to Jerusalem, even though he does not know exactly what will happen there, because he is being "compelled by the Spirit." I would call this the New Testament version of what Nehemiah experienced. Paul says that he is experiencing the compulsion of the Spirit to do a particular thing – in this case, to go to Jerusalem. We do not know if Paul heard an audible voice (he doesn't say so) or if this revelation was delivered in some other way. We do know that Paul considered himself to be bound by the Spirit to go to Jerusalem – he had to go there. There were no other options.

The experience of Paul and Nehemiah in hearing from God through prayer is not unique to them. Certainly their situations were distinct from ours, but their experience of receiving direction from God in prayer is not unique. Believers today are to seek God's face in prayer and be sensitive to his guidance. It just may be the case that God uses your time in prayer to solidify his direction for you. If you have had occasions in your life when you have spent time in prayer over a situation and arose with a suddenly settled sense of what you need to do, then you understand this concept very well. This is why prayer is the starting place for those desiring to know God's direction for where and how they should serve for the sake of His kingdom.

There are, of course, other ways the Bible describes God speaking to us in prayer. One of those ways is through an inner peace (i.e. Is. 26:3, Col. 3:15) that confirms the path God has placed us on. It would seem that God speaks to us in this way most often when we are wrestling with contrasting (or competing) choices. In the context of determining where to serve, having a sense of peace about a given area of ministry may be one of the tools God uses to help you decide between two good opportunities. God also speaks to us in prayer through an inner check (c.f. Acts 27:9-10, 20 and Acts 27:24-26). An inner check is one of the tools God uses when he wants us not to do something. It is the opposite of inner peace. When God puts an inner check in our spirit, the purpose is to keep us from doing a given thing, regardless of how good it may appear. The inner check is a divine disquiet of our soul that says "this is not for you" regardless of how wonderful it may appear to yourself or others.

Of course, it is not possible to exhaust the full number of ways God speaks to us in prayer without mentioning direct revelation. That is exactly what it sounds like – God directly (and perhaps even audibly) telling us to do a given thing. Of course there are a number of biblical passages which demonstrate this: Acts 9:15-16, 22:10, 21, 26:16-20, Galatians 1:11-12, Ephesians 3:3, etc. We want to be very careful with this method of hearing from God, however. Our hearts are so sinful and so often bent toward our own interests that it is easy to mistake our desires for the voice of God. Not to mention the fact that God's revelation of Himself to us in Christ is found in the sixty-six books of the Bible. This means, if you want to be sure you are hearing God's voice, open a Bible and read.

Ask the Lord of the Harvest

While the focus of this book is on helping individual believers discover their place of joyful service in God's Kingdom, such a discovery is not solely an individual process. Church and ministry leadership are called upon to play a key and vital role in helping, nurturing, and mentoring new believers into places of joyful service. So, it is only natural that church and ministry leaders, as well as individual members are called on to pray.

Jesus loved to use everyday situations to teach His disciples deep and abiding lessons. He talked about fishing and agriculture and taxes and anything else that would drive home the point He was making. In Matthew 9, Jesus encounters a large crowd of people who are described as "harassed and helpless, like sheep without a shepherd." In the face of an overwhelming ministry need, Jesus gives His disciples some advice. It is important to remember that these disciples were the people to whom Jesus was going to entrust His ministry. So, the advice He was about to give would set a precedent for them as they wrestled with how to meet future ministry needs.

Matthew 9:37-38 teaches us that, when confronted with ministry needs, Jesus' first piece of advice is to pray. Specifically He tells the disciples "the harvest is plentiful but the workers are few. Ask the Lord of the harvest, therefore, to send out workers into his harvest field." The problem is not a lack of people to minister to, but a lack of people who will minister. So, Jesus says, PRAY!

Consider the teaching of Jesus found in Matthew 9:35-38 (and Luke 10:2). In this passage Matthew writes: [35]Then Jesus went to all the towns and villages, teaching in their synagogues, preaching the good news of the kingdom, and healing every disease and every sickness. [36]When He saw the crowds, He felt compassion for them, because they were weary and worn out, like sheep without a shepherd. [37]Then He said to His disciples, "The harvest is abundant, but the workers are few. [38]Therefore, pray to the Lord of the harvest to send out workers into His harvest." Notice there are at least two principles taught here that are directly applicable to the process of determining how to best serve in God's kingdom. It will be helpful to examine each principle individually.

The first principle is that the needs of the people determine the need for servants. When Jesus has looked at the crowds, He has compassion on them. The text says they are "weary and worn out, like sheep without a shepherd." These are, for

25

the most part, people who have yet to hear the good news of the kingdom. They are people to whom Christ is preaching and ministering. They are not much different than the people we are trying to reach. Jesus describes them as people who are reachable, if there are sufficient workers. I see that in the text when Jesus says that "the harvest is abundant but the workers are few." In Jesus' estimation, the problem is not a lack of people to reach with the gospel; the problem is a lack of people to take the gospel to those who need it.

One of our problems is we compartmentalize ministry into categories that are not based on biblical truth. For example, we look at this text and immediately think Jesus is talking about evangelism or missions. As a result, we think Jesus is asking us to pray for evangelists and missionaries to go share the gospel. But because we do not see ourselves in that role, we do not think the text applies to our service in the local church. After all, what does "the harvest" have to do with serving in the nursery? I would like to propose that every ministry we engage in is to be gospel-driven and tied to the sharing of the gospel. That means that the person working in the nursery has a critical role to play in helping the gospel be proclaimed. They are providing a ministry that allows the parents of young children to have their attention on the preached Word.

Consider that work of "the harvest" includes more than the people who are actually picking the fruit or working in the fields. There are others involved too. Having grown up in an agricultural family, I saw this up close. There were many jobs involved in bringing a crop to harvest, some that took place well before harvest time. There were people who worked to prepare the soil, others to plant the seeds, and still others to keep weeds away. Then at harvest time there were those who picked the crops, those who hauled them back to the trucks and those who took them to market. It would have been a huge mistake (and insult) to only identify the people picking the fruit or harvesting the crops as "workers." We were all workers.

The same is true in God's kingdom. The person serving as a greeter is working to create a friendly environment that helps people feel at ease, so they may hear the gospel. The person handing out bulletins is making sure that people have a sense of what will happen in the service so that they are a bit more at ease, and more open to hear the gospel. The individuals running the audio-video equipment are doing so in order to make sure the gospel is heard clearly – and I mean that literally. In all of these roles (and the dozens more that take place in a church) the work of proclaiming the gospel is our goal. It is the need of people in our generation to hear the gospel that requires servants to serve.

The second principle I see in Matthew 9:35-38 is prayer is the first step in raising up servants. After Jesus notes that the abundance of harvest and the dearth of servants, notice what He says to do: "ask the Lord of the harvest." He tells them to pray. We really ought not be surprised that prayer was Jesus' guidance to the disciples. His entire life and ministry were marked by prayer. Jesus prayed when He was baptized (Lk 3:21), when He was tempted (Heb 5:7-10), when He made major decisions (Lk 6:12-16), when He was performing miracles (Mk 6:41, Jn 11:41-42), and even when He was in agony (Mt 26:36-46, Lk 23:46). Prayer marked Jesus' life and it is only natural that He would urge his disciples to pray when they faced the demands of ministry.

When Jesus tells his disciples to "pray to

the Lord of the harvest to send out workers into His harvest," He is establishing a model that they would ultimately implement in the early church. In Acts 1:14 we find the disciples are gathered in the upper room, waiting on the Holy Spirit. What do they do while they are waiting? They pray. In Acts 1:24 we are told the disciples are preparing to select a replacement for Judas. How do they determine who should fill Judas' spot? They pray. In Acts 6:6 the disciples have been confronted with a ministry dilemma: some of the Grecian Jews are being overlooked in the distribution of food. What do they do? They pray and set apart seven men to take care of the widows while they continue to devote their time to prayer and the Word. In Acts 13:3-4 the church at Antioch is in worship and the Holy Spirit calls them to set apart Paul and Barnabas for the work of ministry. The church leaders laid their hands on them and prayed, and sent them off.

The implication is clear: the early church saturated their decision making with prayer. In particular, when their decisions involved engaging individuals in ministry, they prayed. Of course, they also prayed when deciding ministry strategy (i.e. Acts 16:6-10). Do you notice that the church does not simply wait for individuals to pray, but the church itself is engaged in prayer? The church is intimately involved in the entire process of determining who God is setting apart for a ministry role. The early church engaged in a church-centered approach to filling ministry roles rather than a man-centered (or self-centered) approach. It was the church in prayer. It was the church calling people to serve. It was the church listening for the voice of God. We can only do that if we are a people of prayer.

Following the example of Jesus, church and ministry leadership should pray for the Lord of the harvest to send laborers into the harvest field (Matt 9:38, Lk 10:2). The leadership of the church must begin by asking God, "Who are you raising up to serve to meet the needs of this body?" The individuals that God sets apart to serve should be the result of answered prayer (Acts 6:1-6, 13:1-2).

Final Thoughts

The crew of the fictional *U.S.S. Alabama* experienced confusion, frustration, and a lack of direction because they lost radio communication with central command. I wonder how often believers (and churches) experience the same sort of emotions because we try to figure out how God would have us to serve apart from prayer. Because Jesus taught the first step in finding servants for kingdom work is to pray that the Lord of the harvest would raise them up, Seek God's Face in Prayer is the first step in the *S.U.RV.E.* model.

CHAPTER TWO

Understand Spiritual Gifts:
The New Testament Teaching

While prayer is first and crucial, it must be accompanied by equipping the body through clear biblical teaching about spiritual gifts. Some churches neglect discussions about or teaching on "spiritual gifts" because the topic can be controversial. However, such an approach ignores the task to which the church is called: to equip the saints for the work of ministry (Eph. 4:11).[8]

Who's on First?

"Who's on First?" Just asking the question brings to mind one of the classic comedy sketches of all time. In the sketch, Bud Abbott portrays Dexter Broadhurt, the manager of the fictional St. Louis Wolves baseball team and Lou Costello portrays Sebastion Dinwiddle, a peanut vendor hoping to break into baseball as a catcher. Costello has been cleared to travel with the team and is anxious to know the names of his future teammates. Naturally, he asks Abbott to give him the names of the players so that he can greet them when he joins the team. Unfortunately for Costello – but fortunately for us – the players have rather unique names: Who plays first, What is on second, and I Don't Know plays third base.

The "Who's on First?" routine first began in live burlesque sketches, later moving to live radio broadcasts. In fact, Abbott and Costello performed the routine live on the air several thousand times. The routine has been translated into thirty languages – some of which Abbott and Costello did themselves. The 1945 film *The Naughty Nineties* first gave fans the opportunity to see the routine rather than just hear it.

We all know why the bit is funny: Abbott and Costello are using the same words, but they mean entirely different things. Costello asks "Who?" as a question while Abbott gives "Who" as the answer. And on and on it goes. In the sketch it is funny. When we are thinking about biblical and theological matters, it is not. When it comes to the issue of spiritual gifts, we must be careful to make sure that we are utilizing the same definition of the term.

A Little History

Part of the problem with how we define spiritual gifts has arisen due to the proliferation of spiritual gift identification materials. Prior to the 1960s there is no evidence of any type of written spiritual gift inventory in use. The 1960s, however, proved to be a decade in which a number of psychological instruments were coming into widely accepted use. For example, the Myers–Briggs Type Indicator, which had been in development from the 1940s, began to receive extensive publication in the 1960s.[9] The desire to utilize the tools of social science research for the benefit of the church, combined with the increasing interest in the principles of the Church Growth Movement (CGM) helped lead to the development of the first spiritual gift inventory.

Since 1972, an increasingly large amount of material on the subject of spiritual gifts and spiritual gift identification has been produced.[10] This material includes books, seminars, and spiritual gift inventories (both paper based and online). And why not? Wagner contends that there is no "dimension of the Christian life that more effectively joins the teachings of Scripture with the day-to-day activities of the people of God than spiritual gifts."[11] Thom Rainer, likewise, encourages Christians to discover their spiritual gifts and then use those gifts to build up the body of Christ, which will result in the church growing.[12] In other words, it is fairly well accepted that a believer knowing and operating in their area of spiritual giftedness is indispensable and invaluable to the life of the church. Naturally, a tool to help determine that giftedness would be useful and welcomed.

As the decade of the 1970s gave way to the 1980s, the use of and reliance upon spiritual gift inventories increased. One telling example of the increased reliance upon spiritual gift inventories is found in comparing the material on spiritual gift discovery in two books by Wagner. In 1976, Wagner published *Your Church Can Grow* that included a section entitled "Discovering Your Spiritual Gift" that outlined five steps: explore the possibilities, experiment with as many [gifts] as possible, examine your feelings, evaluate your effectiveness, and expect confirmation from the body.[13] A number of years later, that section was published as a small book; which expanded the "experiment with as many [gifts] as possible" section to include the following injunction:

> One of the best ways to determine which gifs to experiment with first is to go through a spiritual-gifts questionnaire... although a gift inventory like this should not be considered the final word on discovering gifts, it can be very helpful in pointing you in the right direction.[14]

The implication is that, for many, the use of a spiritual gift inventory had become the primary way for an individual to determine where to serve in the life of the local church.

While there is no disputing that spiritual gifts exist or that they are important for the church and believer, if there is a lack of clarity about what is meant by the term "spiritual gifts" we may well end up asking "Who's on First?" We need to make sure we are using the same definition – a biblical definition – of spiritual gifts in order to know what we are supposed to be doing in the life of the church.

The "Conventional View"

Four passages within Paul's writing provide the primary biblical basis from which the conventional view of spiritual gifts is derived: 1 Corinthians 12:8-10, 28-30; Romans 12:6-8, and Ephesians 4:11. Before getting into the details of those texts, it is helpful to define what is meant by the "conventional view" of spiritual gifts. Wagner defines a spiritual gift as "a special attribute given by the Holy Spirit to every member of the Body of Christ, according to God's grace, for use within the context of the Body."[15] Leslie Flynn provides a similar definition when he writes that "a gift is a Spirit-given ability for Christian service."[16] Bruce Bugbee, Don Cousins and Bill Hybels define spiritual gift(s) as "special abilities distributed by the Holy Spirit to every believer according to God's design and grace for the common good of the body of Christ."[17] Other examples could be cited that all utilize a similar definition. [18]

The understanding of the spiritual gifts described in these passages and defined primarily as "divine abilities granted at conversion" has become the conventional view in much of evangelicalism. There are three common elements in the aforementioned definitions: the source of spiritual gifts is the Holy Spirit; the purpose of spiritual gifts is the building up of the Body; and the nature of spiritual gifts as divine abilities granted at a person's conversion. Yet is that what the New Testament teaches? To find out, let's examine each component of the "conventional view."

The Source of Spiritual Gifts

The conventional view understands the Holy Spirit to be the source of spiritual gifts. Paul seemingly cannot be clearer than he is in 1 Corinthians 12:11 where he says, "All these [spiritual gifts] are the work of one and the same Spirit, and he gives them to each one, just as he determines." The Holy Spirit is responsible for the distribution of spiritual gifts among believers, as he determines. The case, it would seem, is closed. The Holy Spirit is the source of spiritual gifts.

It is worth noting, however, that in Romans 12:6 Paul describes spiritual gifts given in accordance with the "grace given us." In the larger context of Romans 12, Paul never mentions the Holy Spirit. He does mention Christ and he mentions "one another," but not the Holy Spirit. If, in fact, the Holy Spirit and spiritual gifts are inseparable, this seems to be a bit peculiar. Further, in Ephesians 4:11 Paul points specifically to Christ as the one who distributes gifts to the body. Once again, in the larger context of Ephesians 4, the Holy Spirit is only mentioned in connection with providing unity. Paul specifically mentions Christ as the giver of spiritual gifts and attributes them, once again, to the "grace [that] has been given."

What are we to make of this? Simply that, for Paul, the discussion of spiritual gifts was far less technical than we would like to make it. Paul did not draw hard and fast lines between the distribution of gifts by the Holy Spirit, by Christ, and as a result of grace. It may well be that Paul described the Holy Spirit as the distributor of spiritual gifts only in 1 Corinthians because it was the church at Corinth that had a skewed understanding of the Holy Spirit's role. Since the church at Corinth emphasized the Spirit's role, Paul adopts their language, but with the corrective that the Holy Spirit not only empowers the spiritual gifts, but He also determines who receives what gift. Ultimately, it would seem, it is enough for Paul to note that the gifts are supernatural in their source. Spiritual gifts come from God, like "every good and perfect gift" (James 1:17a). Keep that in mind. It will have implications later on.

The Purpose of Spiritual Gifts

Much of the literature on spiritual gift discovery acknowledges that "spiritual gifts" are given for the benefit of the body of Christ.[19] The context of the traditionally understood "gift list" passages emphasizes the good of the body as Paul's primary concern. Note the following emphasis on ministry for the benefit of "one another" in the context of the traditional gift list passages:

> So we, though many, are one body in Christ, and individually members *one of another*. (Rom. 12:5, italics mine)

> Love *one another* with brotherly affection. Outdo *one another* in showing honor. Do not be slothful in zeal, be fervent in spirit, serve the Lord . . . Contribute to the needs of the

saints and seek to show hospitality. (Rom. 12: 10-11, 13, italics mine)

To each is given the manifestation of the Spirit *for the common good.* (1 Cor. 12:7, italics mine)

But God has so composed the body, giving greater honor to the part that lacked it, that there may be *no division in the body*, but that the members may have the same *care for one another.* (1 Cor. 12:24-25, italics mine)

On the other hand, the one who prophesies speaks to people for their upbuilding and *encouragement and consolation.* (1 Cor. 14:3, italics mine)

So that the church may be *built up.* (1 Cor. 14:5c, italics mine)

So with yourselves, since you are eager for manifestations of the Spirit, strive to excel in *building up the church.* (1 Cor. 14:12, italics mine)

For you may be giving thanks well enough, but the other person is not being *built up.* (1 Cor. 14:17, italics mine)

Let all things be done for *building up.* (1 Cor. 14:26, italics mine)

So that *all* may learn and *be encouraged* (1 Cor. 14:31, italics mine)

With all humility and gentleness, with patience, bearing with *one another* in love, eager to maintain the *unity* of the Spirit in the bond of peace. (Eph. 4:2-3, italics mine)

To equip the saints for the work of ministry, for *building up the body of Christ*, until we all attain to the *unity* of the faith and the knowledge of the Son of God... (Eph. 4:12-13, italics mine)

When each part is working properly, makes the *body* grow so that it *builds itself up* in love. (Eph. 4:16b)

Thirteen times in the context of these three short sections of Scripture, Paul emphasizes that his primary concern is not an individual finding and exercising his or her abilities, but that the churches to whom he is writing understand that engagement in any ministry must be for the benefit of the body of Christ. The fact that Paul mentions the issue more often in 1 Corinthians is a testament to the circumstances faced by the church at Corinth in which some had become fascinated with outward manifestations of power rather than realizing that such manifestations are meaningless if they do not benefit the body. On that point, Ken Hemphill comments, "the grace gifts of God are designed to edify and enable the body of Christ to advance the kingdom to the ends of the earth."[20]

As if Paul's emphasis on serving for the benefit of "one another" was not enough to make his point, his employment of the body metaphor reinforces that ministry assignments are for the benefit of the body. Note again the repetition of the body metaphor in the context of the traditional gift list passages:

For as in one *body* we have many members, and the members do not all have the same function, so we, though many, are one *body* in Christ, and individually members of one another. (Rom. 12:4-5, italics mine)

For just as the *body* is one and has many members, and all the members of the *body*, though many, are one *body*, so it is with Christ. (1 Cor. 12:12, italics mine)

But God has so composed the *body*, giving greater honor to the part that lacked it, that there may be no division in the *body*, but that the members have the same care for one another. (1 Cor. 12:24-25, italics mine)

Now you are the *body* of Christ and individually members of it. (1 Cor. 12:27, italics mine)

There is one *body* and one Spirit . . . (Eph. 4:4, italics mine)

To equip the saints for the work of ministry, for building up the *body of Christ*, (Eph. 4:12, italics mine)

From whom the whole *body*, joined and held together by every joint with which it is equipped, when each part is working properly, makes the *body* grow so that it builds itself up in love. (Eph. 4:16, italics mine)

Here again, Paul utilizes a consistent metaphor in the context of all three discussions of "spiritual gifts." And like his emphasis on "one another," the church at Corinth receives the greatest number of body metaphor references from Paul. And rightfully so. It was, after all, the church at Corinth that struggled the most with understanding the interconnectedness of believers; an issue the body metaphor addresses directly. Hemphill points out that Paul's emphasis in 1 Corinthians 12 indicates that the Corinthian believers had a "lack of understanding concerning both the appropriate role of gifts and the inherent limitation of gifts."[21] Likewise, Berding observes "in opposition to the Corinthian Christians' self-centered interest in miraculous activities, Paul says that God has placed each believer in roles of ministry for the purpose of edifying his church."[22]

The single greatest unifying theme of all three passages is not the encouragement of individuals to discover their "spiritual gift," but the admonition that gifts are given to benefit the body of Christ; to build others up. D. A. Carson notes that "these gifts are not for personal aggrandizement, but 'for the common good.'"[23] It seems clear that the conventional view has this correct, spiritual gifts are given for the benefit of the body.

The Nature of Spiritual Gifts

To help get a handle on the nature of spiritual gifts, we need to determine two things: why Paul lists the particular gifts that he does in the New Testament and whether there is room for natural abilities to be called "spiritual gifts." We will address the first issue here and the second issue in the next chapter. As mentioned above, there are four passages within Paul's writing that provide the primary biblical basis from which the conventional view of spiritual gifts is derived: 1

Corinthians 12:8-10, 28-30; Romans 12:6-8, and Ephesians 4:11 If we are going to understand why Paul mentions the particular gifts that he does in each list, an examination of a chart of the gift lists is very helpful. Indeed, seeing the lists side by side is quite revealing. Too often we talk about spiritual gifts in isolation from their context within the books that they are found. Below are the gifts that are listed in each passage:

1 Corinthians 12:8-10

- Word of Wisdom
- Word of Knowledge
- Faith
- Healing
- Miracles
- Prophecy
- Discerning of Spirits
- Tongues
- Interpretation

1 Corinthians 12:28-30

- Apostle
- Prophet
- Teaching
- Miracles

- Healing
- Helps
- Administration
- Tongues
- Interpretation

Romans 12:6-8

- Prophecy
- Serving
- Teaching
- Encouragement
- Sharing/Generosity
- Caring/Assisting
- Showing Mercy

Ephesians 4:11

- Apostle
- Prophet
- Evangelist
- Pastor-Teacher

It is obvious that none of the lists are identical. Not a single one of them is an identical match with another. Indeed, the gift lists are distinct from one another in both the number of gifts described as well as the type of gift identified.

Upon closer examination, we find that there is only one kind of gift – related to prophecy – that is found in all four lists. Teaching is found in three of the four. Beyond that, there are no other gifts found in more than two lists. It would seem that if there were a fixed set of spiritual gifts (the way there is for the fruit of the Spirit), we would find identical lists.

Before you think we can simply create a "master list" from these four lists, consider that the four lists are sent to three separate and distinct churches; and each one of those churches was dealing with unique circumstances. Creating a master list from these distinct lists is about as unhelpful as your doctor creating a master list of medications for you to take based on his diagnosis of three or four other patients in his practice. Some of the items may actually be accurate, but many more would be "way off" because the medications are unique to the doctor's diagnosis of those particular patient's conditions. Just as a medical diagnosis is unique to an individual's conditions, the gift lists in the New Testament are as unique as the church's to whom they are sent.

When it comes to spiritual gifts, we tend to overlook the local circumstances that provided the basis for Paul to create the specific lists that he did. What was happening in Corinth that was different from Ephesus? Obviously there was confusion over a particular set of gifts (sometimes called "sign gifts"). To correct their misunderstanding, Paul lists the gifts that they are abusing. Likewise, the church in Ephesus is facing the threat of heresy, which is why Paul emphasizes the gifts that are related to church structure and clear biblical teaching. Rome was not facing an immediate threat from heresy or false understanding about gifts, but was dealing with general disunity between the Jewish and Gentile elements in the church. Thus, Paul's list in Romans is heavy with gifts that emphasize charitable behavior toward one another.

Paul's gift lists are driven, not by trying to educate us about spiritual gifts, as much as addressing specific issues in real local churches. He mentions gifts that are in evidence, need correction, or are useful in those particular churches. That makes tremendous sense, in light of the purpose of spiritual gifts to benefit the body. That is a huge discovery because we tend to default to the exact opposite view. We think that every Christian has been given at least one of the gifts mentioned in one of the lists. We use spiritual gifts tests with static gift lists in churches that are even more different than the churches at Corinth and Ephesus.

Final Thoughts

Misunderstanding a word or phrase because it is used differently than intended can be humorous; "Who's on First?" is a great example of that. But if we are unclear what is meant by biblical and theological terms, confusion can prevail in matters of eternal consequence. The term "spiritual gifts" is just such a term. Spiritual gifts are given by God for the benefit of the body of Christ. But it is unclear how many gifts God has given. That is because the gift lists in Paul's letters are intended to address specific issues within the local congregations to whom he is writing. That is why the lists are different. That is why there is no "master list" of spiritual gifts in the New Testament. In the next chapter we will examine whether natural abilities can be rightly thought of as spiritual gifts.

CHAPTER THREE

Understand Spiritual Gifts:
A Different Approach

We saw in the last chapter that spiritual gifts are given by God for the benefit of the body of Christ. We also saw that the gift lists in the New Testament are not identical because the lists were intended to address the specific issues within the congregation to whom Paul was writing.

The question remains as to what these gifts are. Specifically, are these gifts something that the Holy Spirit grants to a believer upon his or her conversion or is there another explanation? Perhaps the Lord places certain skills (or aptitude for skills), talents, and passions in a person from birth.

Upon his or her conversion, the individual utilizes those skills, talents and passions for the sake of the kingdom. And maybe … just maybe, it is the utilization of those skills, talents and passion that Paul describes as "spiritual gifts."

A Chat with Mom

The significance of an event can often be noted by the phrase: "I remember exactly where I was when ..." For many senior adults hearing about Pearl Harbor might earn that description. For my parent's generation it might be where they were when they heard about the assassination(s) of John F. Kennedy, or Martin Luther King, Jr, or Robert F. Kennedy. For those in my generation the date January 28, 1986 will always be significant. That was the date that the space shuttle Challenger exploded 73 seconds after takeoff. Likewise, for my son's generation (and many others), the date of September 11, 2001 is etched in our memories. In all likelihood, if you were old enough to form memories, you could share where you were when you heard about or witnessed these events.

During my college years, I had one of those events. I remember exactly where I was: standing in a hallway outside the athletic offices of the college I was attending. I was having a phone conversation with my mother – on a phone that hung on the wall with a cord! She was struggling to figure out where to serve in her local church. At the advice of her pastor she had completed a spiritual gift inventory. The results, however, confused her because they did not match up with her passions. Here was a woman who, at that time, had been a believer for over fifteen years and yet had no confidence she was serving faithfully because of the results of a spiritual gift inventory. At some point during the phone call, I remember asking her where she wanted to serve. I asked her what she was good at and how she could utilize that within the church. She said, "you mean I should serve where I want?" and then noted she had not previously thought about spiritual gifts in that fashion. For me, that conversation solidified a growing belief that a lot of people do not serve in the life of the church because they draw strict lines of separation between what they are good at (i.e. how God gifted them from birth) and what they consider "spiritual gifts."

Revisit the Gift Lists

You will remember that earlier I said the idea that spiritual gifts are given "like every good and perfect gift" would have implications later on? It's now, "later on." One of the assumptions often held by those who advocate spiritual gift discovery as essential for Christians to serve effectively is the idea that spiritual gifts are special abilities – spiritual abilities – granted at conversion. After all, when was the last time you heard a pastor or Bible teacher speak of unbelievers possessing "spiritual" gifts? Probably never. Indeed, to do so seems to make no sense. But what is the basis for assuming that spiritual gifts are necessarily granted at conversion? Is it possible that spiritual gifts are more closely related to "natural" abilities than we thought?

To arrive at an answer, we need to revisit the gifts lists found in the New Testament. The reasons for the differences in those lists is a critical piece of evidence in determining the nature of the gifts Paul is talking about. We also need to think in larger – macro – terms about God's purpose in salvation. If his purpose in salvation is "from before the foundation of the world" (Eph. 1:3-14) then it might just be possible that his decision to gift and equip each believer with skills, talents and passions might originate there too. Finally, we need to think about what is meant by "skills, talents, and passions" and how they might be considered a spiritual gift.

Ken Berding has examined Paul's writing in the New Testament to evaluate the nearly one hundred lists that Paul uses in the New Testament.[24] The passages that are traditionally used as "spiritual gift lists" were included in his research. To be considered a list, Berding sought out the occasions where Paul groups together four or more items that could conceivably be considered a list. Berding's purpose was to determine if the gift list passages were unique from the rest of the lists Paul had created. His findings are very interesting. Berding makes six observations about Paul's use of lists that are significant; they are as follows:

1. Paul uses lists in every letter he writes (except Philemon).
2. Paul's lists include virtue lists, vice lists, qualifications lists, doxologies, and confessional statements that in some cases may have already been in use before he used them.
3. A clear majority of Paul's lists appear to have been created by him for the particular needs and issues he was addressing as he wrote.
4. The words in a list may all be in the same

grammatical form, or may be in mixed grammatical forms.

5. Lists are not arbitrary. A concept or theme always holds them together.

6. Paul regularly and repeatedly indicates the nature of his list. In the majority of cases (around 80 percent) in which he creates or uses a list, he somewhere besides in the list itself uses explicit words to identify what unifies the components of the list.[25]

The significance of Berding's work is that it sheds light on what holds the traditional "gift lists" together. The conventional view has been that each of the four traditional gift lists fits under an overarching umbrella of "spiritual gifts," which are typically defined as "abilities" or "attributes" given to the believer by the Holy Spirit at conversion, for use within the body of Christ. In other words, the conventional view sees these four traditional gift list passages providing a list of divinely given abilities. As a result, spiritual gift inventories have utilized a composite of the four passages to create a list of gifts to test. To create a composite list, however, ignores significant differences in the churches to whom Paul was writing. It is to those differences that we now turn in order to find an answer to what really holds those gift lists together.

The Influence of Historical Setting

Each gift list in the New Testament has unique characteristics that are influenced by the circumstances in the local church itself.[26] In examining the gift list passages in 1 Corinthians, Romans, and Ephesians, one notes significant differences in the number and type of gifts represented. These differences are not incidental, but are the result of specific historical concerns in each respective church. First Corinthians, for example, contains two lists of gifts. The first list is in 1 Corinthians 12:8-10 and contains extraordinary (sometimes called, "charismatic") gifts, while the second listing of gifts in 1 Corinthians 12:28 contains seven gifts, including five gifts of a more reserved nature that were not mentioned in the list in vv. 8-10: apostle, prophet, teachers, helps and administrators. Hemphill argues that the difference in these two lists is intentional and driven by Paul's concern over the "spirituals" in Corinth who were using their exercise of ecstatic gifts as "proof of their advanced spirituality."[27] Thus, it would be an error to merge the two lists into one list of possible spiritual gifts, when, in fact, the lists were being used to broaden the Corinthians understanding of spiritual gifts.[28]

When considering the context of 1 Corinthians 12, it is essential to keep in mind the overall context of the first letter to the church at Corinth. Even a cursory reading of 1 Corinthians will demonstrate that the church at Corinth was a church filled with divisions and factions. Early in the letter, Paul takes the church to task for their alignment with certain personalities. His assessment of their condition in 1 Corinthians 1:10-12 is quite revealing: I appeal to you, brothers, by the name of our Lord Jesus Christ, that all of you agree with one another so that there may be no divisions among you, and that you be perfectly united in mind and thought. My brothers, some from Chloe's household have informed me that there are quarrels among you. What I mean is this: One of you says, "I follow Paul," another "I follow Apollos," another "I follow Cephas," still another, "I follow Christ."

D. A. Carson points out that as the content of 1 Corinthians unfolds, it appears that Paul is striving to work out mediating principles for the church that will ensure their unity.[29] These mediating principles extend to a number of issues including the exercise of spiritual gifts. It seems that in Corinth there were those who experienced envy and jealousy over the gifts exercised by others. Others seem to have been intimidated by the exercise of certain gifts to the point that they were either excluded or withdrew from the body (see especially, 1 Cor. 12:14-26). Thus, it is the emphasis on unity – driven by the division created by the exercise of certain gifts –that plays a significant role in the gifts mentioned in the letter to Corinth.

The context of Romans in general and Romans 12 in particular, demonstrates a similar, but different problem of disunity in that church from that which faced the church at Corinth. The problem in Rome was different from that in Corinth in that the problem in Rome was driven primarily by the ethnic divide between Jews and Gentiles. Thomas Schreiner argues that Paul's effort to resolve this ethnic division was one of the reasons he wrote the letter to Rome.[30]

This purpose for writing Romans becomes clear early in the book, as Paul describes the gospel by saying: "For I am not ashamed of the gospel, for it is the power of God for salvation to everyone who believes, to the Jew first and also to the Greek" (Rom. 1:16). Further, Paul argues that both alike are under sin when he writes: "What then? Are we Jews any better off? No, not at all. For we have already charged that all, both Jews and Greeks, are under sin." (Rom 3:9). The theme of unity between Jews and Gentiles appears again in Romans 4:9ff., 7:1ff., 9:1-11:36, and later in 14:1-15:33. In the midst of these latter and longer two sections (Rom. 9:1-11:36 and 14:1-15:33), one finds a short section (Rom. 12:3-8) that emphasizes the importance of unity, despite a diversity of gifts. The placement of these verses is intended to emphasize that the exercise of spiritual gifts should not be separated from the unity of the body.[31]

Regarding spiritual gifts, Hemphill considers Rome to be the "control" situation, as there is not a specific threat to orthodoxy or orthopraxy.[32] In Romans 12:6-8 there is no mention of the extraordinary gifts, so the problem in Corinth is clearly not in view, but rather the emphasis instead is on leadership and service gifts. If Rome is the control situation, the fact that only gifts of leadership and service are mentioned is significant as it reflects those gifts as priorities in Paul's mind in the absence of a specific problem related to spiritual gifts to address.

Scholars disagree as to the occasions and purpose for the writing of Ephesians.[33] Rudolf Schnackenburg, however, argues that Paul's concern over two basic issues led to the writing of Ephesians: "the internal unity of the congregation ... and ... a distinctly Christian way of life" which is set apart from the larger world.[34] If Schnackenburg is correct, a purpose for writing Ephesians emerges that is related to the issue of the unity of the church in Ephesus. Such an emphasis presupposes that there is something causing (or may cause) disunity in the body.

While it may be impossible to be dogmatic about the precise threat to unity, it seems reasonable that the unity of the church is a dominant theme of the letter.[35] Concerning spiritual gifts, the emphasis in Ephesians is on leadership, teaching, and service gifts, which seems most likely to be in response to the "unique needs created by the threat of false teaching."[36]

Indeed, Hemphill notes that "Ephesians 4 is the only text in which Paul connects the use of the gifts to the maintenance of doctrinal stability."[37] Paul reminds the Christians in Ephesus that genuine unity flows from a deep and abiding love for Christ, who has provided gifts to his body so that it may grow to full maturity.

Different Gifts in Different Settings

The possibility of local circumstantial influence is significant, for if the gifts exist as individual abilities apart from the life of the church, one might expect to find a more static list, such as the fruit of the Spirit (Gal. 5:22-23). If the gift lists, however, are influenced by the circumstances within the local church, there is significant question as to whether or not the gifts are intended to be static.[38] So, what is the glue that holds the spiritual gift lists together?

Berding argues that Paul indicates what each of the lists in the four traditional gift list passages have as their conceptual glue.[39] In Ephesians 4, the conceptual glue is the phrase "for the equipping of the saints." Thus, the content of the Ephesians 4 list is concerned with a list of equippers God has chosen to bestow upon the Church. In Romans 12, the primary conceptual glue seems to be the idea of functions and members in those functions, found in verse 4, which reads "and all the members do not have the same function." First Corinthians 12:27-31 contains the phrase "And God has placed/appointed in the church" (v. 28), which, when taken together with the overarching body metaphor in verse 27, reveals a conceptual glue of appointments or placements. In 1 Corinthians 12:7-11, the conceptual glue is found in v. 7: "But to each one is give the manifestation of the Spirit." The list that follows is a list of activities that manifest the Spirit.

In every case above, the gift list is held together not by the conceptual theme of specially gifted individuals. Rather, the conceptual glue is intimately tied to the circumstances within the local church that Paul argues God has provided for through various ministries. For the church at Corinth, he points out manifestations of the Spirit (1 Cor. 12:7-10) and ministry appointments (1 Cor. 12:28-30). To believers in Ephesus, Paul emphasizes equippers of the body to maintain orthodoxy (Eph. 4:11-13) and to those in Rome, his focus is on members serving in various ministry functions (Rom. 12:6-8).

Wagner himself holds that the gift lists are not intended to be exhaustive, but are "representative of gifts the Holy Spirit brought to the mind of the biblical writer" at the time the text was written.[40] Hemphill also concludes that "the lists were never intended to be *comprehensive* but only *illustrative* of the sort of abilities God might give an individual that would enable him or her to serve the King of kings acceptably" (italics his).[41] If the gift lists are representative of possible gifts, then the enablement of the Spirit may vary from one congregation to another.

If, in fact, the gifting of the Spirit is in keeping with the needs and circumstances of the individual congregation, is it possible for an individual to exercise different "gifts" depending upon the congregation in which they find themselves? If individuals do exercise different "gifts" depending on the needs of the congregation, is it even appropriate to talk about "gifts" as individual possessions at all? It seems more appropriate to describe the "gifts" in terms of ministries or functions within the body rather than individually possessed "abilities" that may be moved around at the will of the individual. Further, the fact that the listing of spiritual gifts is apparently driven more by the needs within the church itself rather than a static, terminal list of gifts from which Paul may select, provides a clue as to the larger nature and purpose of God for spiritual gifts.

A Bigger Picture

Although it is clear that the gifts lists are driven by the circumstances in each local church, the question of whether natural abilities can be considered spiritual gifts has not been answered. There is, in fact, something of an intramural theological debate over how close a relationship there is between natural abilities and spiritual gifts. Edmund Clowney, for example, comments that "in advancing the work of the Spirit, we cannot sharply separate natural gifts from spiritual gifts."[42] While Wagner recognizes that God may take a natural talent and transform it when that person becomes a follower of Christ, he warns against confusing natural talents with spiritual gifts.[43] The result? On the one hand we hear we ought not sharply separate natural abilities and spiritual gifts. On the other hand we are warned against seeing them too closely aligned. Yet both sides acknowledge that simply because a person is a good public school teacher, he or she has the spiritual "gift" of teaching. No wonder there is confusion over spiritual gifts.

To arrive at an answer, we need to "back up" just a bit. That is, when we get focused on spiritual gifts, we immediately begin to think about "abilities granted at conversion." We need to get a larger, broader view of God's purpose and then examine the more specific issue of spiritual gifts. It is safe to say that all gifts come from God. Even when we talk about "natural talents" we often describe them as "God given." And we are right. Remember what James said, "every good and perfect gift" comes from the Father. So, in the broadest sense, every gifting that we possess has God as its source.

Further, the God who made us also knew we would come to faith and that he had a purpose for us in the kingdom. This is not a new concept, but a really old one. Think, for example, about Isaiah, Jeremiah, and John the Baptist – to name a few. God set each of these men apart – from birth – for special tasks. Although the role of the Holy

Spirit in a believer's life is different after Pentecost, that has not altered God's attributes. He is still omniscient, omnipotent, and omnipresent. He still has an eternal purpose that He is working out in the world. Is it, then, unusual to think that God would still gift and equip men and women that he intends to use in his kingdom from birth?

Skills, Talents, and Passions

Because there is not static (or exhaustive) list of spiritual gifts in the New Testament, and because every gift comes from God (including our skills, talents, and passions), and because God has an eternal, kingdom-focused purpose for investing those skills, talents and passions in every believer, it is clear we need a different way of defining spiritual gifts. Based on the evidence from the New Testament gift lists and the plain teaching of the Bible about God's eternal purpose for believers, it seems best to define the term spiritual gifts as "an individual's God-given skills, talents and passions willingly used to serve and benefit the body of Christ in order to advance the Kingdom of God."

In this definition, the clear purpose of spiritual gifts (as examined in chapter two) is maintained; namely, the benefit of the body. But what is unique here is that a person's conversion is not necessarily considered the place at which a gift is granted. Rather, it is at / after conversion that a person is willing to take their God-given gifts and utilize them for the sake of God's kingdom. That is, "their" gifts are recognized to really be theirs only in the sense of stewardship. In that light, those gifts are brought under the Lordship of Christ to be used in the advance of God's kingdom. Thus, in this view, the focus is not on the timing of the gifts, but what a person does with the skills, talents, and passions God has invested in him or her for the sake of the kingdom.

Practically this means that, rather than ask a believer to take a spiritual gift inventory to determine where they should serve, we might do better to ask: What are you good at? What do you enjoy doing? What are your passions? What skill set do you possess? Church leaders then match those answers up with the needs of the congregation. This concept will be explored more – including definitions of "skills, talents, and passions' – in the next chapter.

Final Thoughts

Rethinking our understanding of spiritual gifts can be challenging. A large number of Christians have assumed a definition of spiritual gifts without ever examining the context of the gift list passages or the larger purpose of God in salvation. As a result, many believers have grown frustrated at trying to figure out where to serve in the life of the church. Many, like my mom, took a spiritual gift test only to end up more confused. Church leaders would do well to step back and rethink such a process. Giving a spiritual gift test is easy. The harder work is to walk a person through the path of discipleship to the point that they understand that all of their skills, talents, and passions are to be brought under the Lordship of Christ.

In case you were wondering, after our conversation about spiritual gifts, my mom began to pursue her passion by leading a number of Precept Bible studies. In the 20 years since that conversation, she has impacted the lives of hundreds of women by utilizing her God-given skills, talents, and passions rather than relying on the results of a spiritual gift inventory alone. Hers is only one story, but I suspect it is a story that can be repeated hundreds of thousands of times in the lives of believers.

CHAPTER FOUR

Regularly Volunteer

The journey to discover your place of joyful service within God's kingdom begins with prayer. The next step that many people are encouraged to take is to figure out their spiritual gifts. The previous two chapters have examined the New Testament teaching on spiritual gifts in detail. The conclusion is that spiritual gifts are not as mysterious as you may have thought. Indeed, spiritual gifts were summarized in the last chapter as "an individual's God-given skills, talents and passions willingly used to serve and benefit the body of Christ in order to advance the kingdom of God." That is a very freeing idea – using whatever gifts God has given you for the sake of His kingdom. Yet too often our churches create barriers to individuals serving. The goal of this chapter is to share some ways to recognize those barriers and respond to them. Ultimately, I hope to give you some solid ways to get involved in the life of your church.

A Picture of the Church

In terms of average attendance, the National Football League is the most well attended sports league in the world. With an average attendance of more than 67,000 people per game, the NFL easily outpaces all other team sports (except auto racing). What that means is that a lot of people enjoy watching others play football. It is a pretty good guess that many of the people in the stands watching a football game have actually played the game at some point in their lives. Perhaps it was a backyard game of "touch' football or maybe they played in an Upward flag football league. Given that over 250,000 youths participate in Pop Warner Youth Football and that more than 1 million play high school football every year, it is likely that many NFL spectators have actually played a down of real, tackle football.

Yet they are content to sit back and watch the game on Sunday. It's not as if those in the stands couldn't use the exercise. We are seemingly constantly reminded by the media (and our doctors) how out of shape and overweight most Americans are. Considering that somewhere in the neighborhood of 20 million hot dogs will be consumed by those fans during the course of the season, it is clear that getting in shape is not the primary motivator for being at the game. No, watching the professionals play the game is why the fans show up. They want to watch someone else play.

I once heard that the church is a lot like an NFL game. At any given NFL game there are – on average – nearly 70,000 fans in dire need of exercise watching twenty-two men in dire need of rest. That, too often, is a picture of the church. Pastors and church leaders clamor for volunteers. The children's director is exasperated at the number of kids attending and the lack of workers. The worship leader is frustrated that he cannot get a guitarist (or pianist or more choir members) to serve on a regular basis. The pastor's heart breaks because he sees new families visit weekly, yet few get plugged into the life of the church. There are plenty of places to serve, but it does not appear that many people are aware of that fact.

Regardless the size church you are a part of (or are leading), the dearth of people to serve is very real. I have been privileged to serve in three distinct settings. One was a small rural church of less than one hundred attenders. The next was a larger setting of about one hundred fifty. I currently serve in a "mid-size" church of about five hundred. Every time I transitioned from one to the other I thought the issue of raising up volunteers would get easier. It did not. It is as challenging to get volunteers to serve in a church of five hundred as it was in a church of seventy-five.

Joe Knows Guitar

Consider this scenario. Joe is a man in his mid-40s who begins attending your church. He enjoys the sermon, the friendliness of the people and his kids love the children's ministry. He particularly likes the music. He grew up in a church that had an organ on one side and a piano on the other. Back then the songs were lead by a well meaning lady who couldn't carry a tune in a bucket. But here, in your church, he hears guitars and drums and quality vocalists. This matters to him because he spent years playing in cover bands during his "younger days." Now, Joe is a bit older, but can still play the guitar pretty well. He is as good as the players in your church.

Joe thinks he might want to join the band, but he faces two problems. First, he does not know how to go about joining the band. He does not hear announcements about auditions and there is nothing in the worship program about how to start serving. Second, Joe hears the pastor encourage people to "discover their spiritual gift" so they can serve in the church. He is not sure that his ability to play a Stratocaster is a spiritual gift. It did not seem like one when he was playing in the bars back in his college days. So, Joe leaves church discouraged because he is unable to serve God with the one thing he is really good at.

This scenario is real. It has played out in at least two churches that I have served personally. I suspect that it happens on a weekly basis in churches all across America. So, before we delve into what it means to "regularly volunteer," let me say a few words to church leaders. I am convinced that we have sent too many confusing messages to the folks in our churches, many of whom are ready, eager, and willing to serve. They simply do not know what we want them to do. As church leaders, we bear the responsibility to make clear how Christ-followers can find their place of joyful service in the kingdom.

Two Ditches to Avoid

Many churches (and church leaders) tend to fall into one of two ditches when it comes to seeking volunteers to serve in the life of the church. The first is the ditch of making service too difficult to enter into. We establish far too many levels of bureaucracy for people to wade through before they can actually begin serving.

If you have been in very many churches, you will be familiar with the scenario. Sally joins the church and is excited to be a part of her new church family. She wants to get plugged in and start serving. In her previous church she taught children's Sunday school, sang in the choir and helped out on the benevolence committee. Sally is directed to the chair of the nominating committee. She is thanked for her desire to get involved, but all the slots from the nominating committee are filled for this year. The choir, which usually accepts folks all year, has been working on the big Easter musical and the worship leader is not sure this would be a good time for her to join. Perhaps after Easter, she is told. In the best case scenario, she sits back and waits. In the worst case scenario, she leaves the church to find a place she can be more useful.

An exaggeration? Maybe. Maybe not. The reality is we can unwittingly create an unscalable wall of bureaucracy by our organization. Organization must always encourage ministry. It should undergird and support ministry, not restrict it to a handful of people. We must build clear and simple pathways for people to follow as they engage in ministry. A good test? If someone walked up to you and asked "how can I get involved in the ministry of your church?" Would you have an answer? If not, how long would it take you to get one? Do you have places for people to immediately begin serving? If not, you may have a bloated bureaucracy.

The second ditch we fall into is the ditch of making service too insignificant to enter. It really is the opposite of the first ditch. While the first ditch makes serving too difficult, at least it give the impression that serving in the life of the church is a big deal. This second ditch has the opposite effect.

Often in reaction to the first ditch, some church leaders decide to make serving "as easy as possible." We ask people to serve "just once a month" or, worse yet, once per quarter. As we are describing the ministry options we use words like easy, simple, and very little preparation required. Although our intentions are good, the result is that we set the bar for serving way too low. In so doing, we invariably give the impression that the ministry we are asking people to engage in is just not that important. After all, if it is easy, requires little preparation and I only have to serve once per quarter, how critical can it be?

Although we may involve more people more quickly, the "easy as possible" approach inevitably backfires. We unintentionally give the impression that the role we are asking people to fulfill in the life of the church is insignificant. It is easy to walk away from a commitment that costs little and means less. The simple truth is, the lower we set the bar of expectations for serving, the less seriously people will take it.

It is clear that a balance is necessary. Church leaders need to have clear expectations and responsibilities for the various places of service in the church. Every "job" in the church fulfills a part of the gospel being proclaimed in that place. Paul affirms in 1 Corinthians 12:14-26 that there are no unimportant places of service in the body of Christ. Every job matters and is critical to that local church carrying out the call of God to proclaim the gospel in that place. At the same time, we cannot make the pathway to service so difficult that one's fire to serve burns out before he or she is allowed to serve. So the pathway to service needs to be simple and easy to navigate. The responsibilities and expectations for service need to be high; consistent with the gospel-critical nature of serving in the church.

Remove the Mystery

One final word needs to be said to church leaders before we explore the details of regularly volunteering. That word is simply this: remove the mystery of serving. Over the past forty years or so local churches have become enamored with using the phrase "serve in your area of spiritual giftedness." We hear sermons where pastors expound on the spiritual gift passages and encourage you to "put your gift to work in the church." Like Joe, many contemporary church-goers are left shaking their heads. They are not sure what a spiritual gift is, if they have one, and if so, how to use it. Or, worse yet, we strain credulity with our people by trying to define a talent (like guitar playing) into a pre-determined spiritual gift category (like "encouragement"). His guitar playing may be encouraging, but it is highly unlikely that Paul had shredding a guitar in mind when he wrote about "encouragement." In my estimation, this is part of the language of Zion that needs to either be explained more clearly, or discarded.

By embracing the definition of spiritual gifts shared in the previous chapter – "an individual's God-given skills, talents and passions willingly used to serve and benefit the body of Christ in order to advance the kingdom of God" – we can remove much of the mystery of what it means to serve Christ. Using this definition we can tell a guy like Joe that his willingness to give his talent (and skill and passion) away for the sake of the kingdom IS his spiritual gift to the church. Rather than using that talent to make money, his heart is transformed and now that talent is a tool to bring glory to God.

Where to Begin

As a follower of Christ you have been called

to serve in your local church. One of the clear teachings from 1 Corinthians 12 is that every believer has been called to participate in the body of Christ. Every believer has a part to play in the church's effort to fulfill the Great Commission. Indeed, Paul writes in 1 Corinthians 12:18 that "God has arranged the parts in the body, every one of them, just as he wanted them to be." That means that God has placed you in the church you are in for a purpose. He has you there to make a difference by using the skills, talents, and passions He placed within you.

Many who subscribe to the conventional view of spiritual gift discovery draw a sharp distinction between birth gifts and spiritual gifts. But as has been shown, such a sharp distinction is not necessary. The few items described in the spiritual gifts lists in 1 Corinthians, Romans and Ephesians that are necessarily post-conversion, are those gifts used to validate the gospel in the apostolic age.[44] The vast majority of the gifts listed in those passages are not necessarily post-conversion. Ken Hemphill, a noted scholar on the subject of spiritual gifts, makes the argument that some spiritual gifts may be "birth gifts that are transformed by the Spirit."[45] His argument has seven component parts:

1. We are created by God with unique purpose and design.
2. Our life experiences and opportunities become a part of God's benevolent gift to us that shapes our entire person.
3. At some point we experience spiritual birth that is accompanied by the transformation of our bodies, enabling all the members of our body to be of use in kingdom service (Rom. 6:12-13). Birth gifts may become spiritual gifts.
4. With conversion our spiritual blindness is removed, and we receive the Spirit so that we may know the things freely given to us by God (1 Cor. 2:12).
5. As believers we present our bodies to the Lord as a living sacrifice, acceptable to God, as our spiritual service of worship (Rom. 12:1).
6. The empowering of the Spirit transforms all of our abilities and life experiences, enabling us to serve God effectively.
7. We can now accomplish the good works God prepared for us before we were

conceived.[46]

This concept opens up a whole new world to people desiring to serve in the church. Rather than taking a spiritual gift inventory or trying to struggling to decipher their "spiritual gift," this approach allows a person to begin with something that is known. To help you better understand where to begin let me define what is meant by "skills, talents, and passion."

Skills refer to any ability that one has acquired either through training or life experience. It may or may not be connected to a "natural talent." The idea of a skill being the result of God's blessing or used in kingdom service is not new. Just a few biblical examples will suffice to demonstrate that skills are essential in kingdom life. One of my favorites is Kenaniah. This man is only mentioned three times in the Old Testament (1 Chron. 15:22,27; 26:29). It is the first occasion that is of interest. In 1 Chronicles 15 King David is assembling leaders and musicians to celebrate the return of the ark of the covenant to Jerusalem. In 1 Chronicles 15:22 we are told that Kenaniah was "in charge of the singing." Why? Why was he put in the charge of the singing? Because he was skillful at it.

Talent refers to those things for which we have a natural affinity. Certainly there may be overlap between skills and talents, but there is a difference. For example, think of the folks in your church who have a tremendous singing voice. Is there training involved in a person developing a good singing voice? Sure. But some of us – and I would be at the front of the line – could receive all the training in the world and still not have a great singing voice. My sister, on the other hand, has a tremendous voice. She always has, even at 12 years old when she sang at my wedding. She has trained her voice in the years since, but no one would mistake her training for the fact that she has a natural talent in that area.

I like to define *passion* as the thing that makes your heart sing. Confucius once said, choose a job you love and you will never have to work a day in your life. He is tapping into the idea of passion. Passion is the thing that we are willing to do whether we get paid or not. It is the thing that we often pour money into simply because we love to do it. My guess is that I do not have to tell you what you are passionate about. Most of us know immediately. If we failed to follow Confucius' advice, it is the thing we think about when our job is not going well. Another way to determine your passion is to look at your checkbook. Jesus said that where our treasure is, there our heart will be also (Mt. 6:21). Our money always ends up where our heart is.

How can you use your passion in ministry? There once was a couple in a church I served that decided to take up sailing. Neither one had much experience with sailing, but with the kids grown and out of the house, they wanted something they could do together. They ended up purchasing a sailboat and taking sailing lessons. It didn't take long for them to realize that they had developed a passion for sailing. More than that, they developed a heart for the friends they met while sailing. When I met them they shared that they were gone most weekends during "the season." As they told me the story about their love of sailing they said, "It did not take long for us to realize we had to use this passion to reach people for Jesus." There it is! Sailing may not be on the typical spiritual gift list, but using one's love of sailing to introduce people to Jesus is certainly a tool for the kingdom.

An Old Testament Example

When the children of Israel were constructing the Tabernacle, we have a fascinating look at how God interweaves skills, talents and passions. In Exodus 35 and 36 we read the account of Bezalel and Oholiab, the men responsible for the craftsmanship of the Tabernacle. Listen to how they are described in Exodus 35:30-36:2:

Then Moses said to the Israelites, "See, the LORD has chosen Bezalel son of Uri, the son of Hur, of the tribe of Judah, and he has filled him with the Spirit of God, with *skill*, *ability* and *knowledge* in all kinds of crafts-- to make *artistic designs* for work in gold, silver and bronze, to cut and set stones, to work in wood and to engage in all kinds of artistic craftsmanship. And he has given both him and Oholiab son of Ahisamach, of the tribe of Dan, the *ability to teach others.* He has filled them with *skill* to do all kinds of work as *craftsmen*, *designers*, *embroiderers* in blue, purple and scarlet yarn and fine linen, and weavers--all of them *master craftsmen* and *designers.* So Bezalel, Oholiab and every *skilled* person to whom the LORD has given *skill* and *ability* to know how to carry out all the work of constructing the sanctuary are to do the work just as the LORD has commanded." Then Moses summoned Bezalel and Oholiab and every *skilled* person to whom the LORD had given *ability* and who was *willing* to come and do the work (italics mine).

This passage is remarkable and it coheres remarkably well with the understanding of spiritual gifts proposed in this book. There is no question that God is the source of Bezalel and Oholiab's "gifts." But do you notice how those gifts are described? They are skill, ability, and knowledge as craftsmen, designers, and embroiderers. These are the kind of "gifts" that come after years of training and, likely, apprenticeship. I suspect we have Bezalel's and Oholiab's in churches all around us who have no idea that their skill in craftsmanship, accounting, web design, computer networking, photography, interior design, or a myriad of other things are exactly what God would have them use in the church.

It is reasonable to assume that Bezalel, Oholiab, and some of those who came to work had a talent for such work. This is especially so when we consider the artistic nature of the work. The arts typically require some natural talent in order to perform well. And then, consider the question of passion. The final verse describes the people working with Bezalel and Oholiab as "willing" to come and do the work. What would make you willing? Passion; not only the passion of the workers, but the passion of their leaders.

Indeed, the final verse is a great summation of utilizing your skills, talents, and passion ... all three are mentioned in the verse. Look at Exodus 35:2 again: "Then Moses summoned Bezalel and Oholiab and every *skilled* person to whom the LORD had given *ability* and who was *willing* to come and do the work (italics mine)." The verse describes skilled people, with ability (talent) from the Lord who are willing (because of passion) to come and do the work. We are the ones who have created an unhealthy (and I would argue, unbiblical) distinction between spiritual gifts and the skills, talents and passion God implanted in an individual.

FAT – A Good Motivator

Let's assume that you are convinced that giving away your skills, talents, and passion for the sake of the kingdom is the way God intends for you to serve. Perhaps you have decided that the way we have traditionally understood spiritual gifts is more restrictive than the Holy Spirit intended. There remains the question of motivation. Thinking back to the opening illustration of the football stadium, what is it that will get you out of the stands and on the field? The acronym FAT seems to be a consistent biblical motivator to service. FAT is an acronym for **F**orgiven, **A**vailable, **T**eachable.

The story of Isaiah the prophet's encounter with God in the year that King Uzziah died (Is. 6:1-9a) provides the framework for FAT. Isaiah goes to the temple, ostensibly to mourn his friend, the king, who died in disgrace. While in the temple, Isaiah has a profound encounter with God. The veil of heaven is pulled back and Isaiah gets a glimpse of the throne room of heaven. As the angels sing "Holy, holy, holy is the LORD Almighty, the whole earth is filled with his glory" Isaiah sees (and feels) the temple shaking. Even the inanimate doorposts and thresholds of the temple quake in the presence of Almighty God. Isaiah does too. He quakes because he realizes his sinfulness. What happens next provides the framework for FAT.

Forgiven

When Isaiah recognizes his sinfulness, he confesses his sins – noting especially his mouth. Perhaps in light of God's glory, Isaiah realizes how far short he has fallen in speaking of God. Once he confesses, an angel takes a coal from the altar and touches it to his lips, the very place Isaiah has identified as sinful. The angel then announces "your guilt is taken away and your sin atoned for." Isaiah is forgiven.

Biblically speaking, the nearly universal response of one who has been forgiven is to serve. Jesus taught this very principle. In Luke 7:36-50 he is at the home of a Pharisee having dinner. A woman who lived a sinful life comes in and kneels at his feet. She is weeping so much that his feet are wet, so she wipes them with her hair and then pours perfume on them. The Pharisee is incensed. How could a respectable rabbi allow such a sinful woman to touch him in this manner? So Jesus tells a story about two men who owed a debt to the same man. One of them had an insurmountable debt, while the other had only a minor debt. They both had their debts forgiven. Jesus then asks the Pharisee, which one will love the man who canceled the debt more? The Pharisee responds that the one who was forgiven more. Then Jesus taught a principle: One who has been forgiven much, loves much. The one forgiven little loves little. Notice that forgiveness results in love; love that moves a person to action.

Paul teaches the same principle in a different way. In 2 Corinthians 5:14, 18-19 Paul teaches that we are compelled by Christ's love to take the gospel to others. He says that – because we have been forgiven – we should no longer live for ourselves, but for Him who died for us and was raised again. He then says that once we were reconciled, we were given a ministry of reconciliation. The principle here is simple: if you are forgiven, you are to love by your actions. If you are forgiven, you have been reconciled and are now in the ministry of reconciliation ... no option. You are in the ministry!

Available

Returning to Isaiah 6, consider that Isaiah's response to the angel's announcement of forgiveness is met with an immediate willingness to serve. Immediately after hearing that glorious announcement, God asks, "Who will go for us? Who shall we send?" Isaiah's immediate reaction to knowing God had a job that needed to be done was to volunteer. He responds to the Lord by saying, "Here am I. Send me!"

It has been pointed out countless times that Isaiah's response is not one of identifying his location. He did not say, "Here I am" as if God had no idea where to find him. Rather, he said, "Here am I." That is a statement of availability. Not only is he available, but he is willing. "Send me," he says.

Isaiah puts no conditions on his service. He is simply available. He does not inquire as to whether God is calling him to do something safe, secure, convenient, or costly. Instead, Isaiah offers a blank check. "Here am I. Send me." Send you where, Isaiah? It doesn't matter. Send you to do what? It doesn't matter. Whatever the One who forgave me wants, I will do. That is the response of one who is forgiven, I am available. Use me.

Teachable

Being forgiven and available does not mean we already know everything about serving. As soon as Isaiah offers himself to God's service, God begins to teach him what it is he would have Isaiah do. And Isaiah willingly receives direction and instruction from the Lord. He is teachable. God tells him what to do. Isaiah interacts and receives clarification. But he is not stiff-necked nor is he prideful; nor does he think he knows better than God. No. He is open to receiving God's instruction and direction.

For most of us who serve God's kingdom by serving in a local church, we will receive that instruction and direction from our spiritual leaders. Our pastors, elders, deacons, Sunday school teachers, small group leaders, and fellow servants will all pour into our lives. They will teach us and guide us into how to serve most effectively. Our task is to remain open to how God may choose to use us and teachable toward those tasked with leading us toward spiritual maturity.

Final Thoughts

So, are you in the stands or are you on the field? Is there a ministry in your local church that could not function if you were not serving? If not, remember that God has invested tremendous skills, talents, and passions in you. He has called you to faith in Christ and now wants you to use those skills, talents, and passions in service for His Kingdom. My guess is you already have a pretty good idea of the kind of things you can do to serve the Lord. Once you move beyond the conventional understanding of a limited number of spiritual gifts given at your conversion to the wide open perspective of a sovereign God investing all sorts of skills, talents, and passions in you from the very beginning, the sky is the limit.

In addition, when you consider the great mercy of God in drawing you to Himself, to forgiving your sins in Christ, and to making you a new creation, the response is to serve. Not to earn God's favor – we already have that in Christ – but to demonstrate God's worth by giving our skills, talents, and passions away for the sake of his Kingdom. In so doing, we remain available to however God wants to use us and we maintain a teachable disposition toward those spiritually responsible for our growth. The best way to get off the field and in the game is to use your skills, talents, and passion. And remember – stay FAT.

CHAPTER FIVE

Evaluate Effectiveness

So, you have prayed, you have examined your skills, talents and abilities, you recognize your willingness to give away your skills, talents and passion as a spiritual gift, and you have begun to serve. Now what? What is the next step to ensure you are serving in such a way to advance God's kingdom and to bring joy to your own heart and life? Quite simply, it is necessary to evaluate your effectiveness.

"The Annual Review"

"How was your day, honey?" I innocently asked my wife. Susy has been a nurse for nearly ten years. And a quite good one, if I may say so. She currently works in the recovery room for patients who have undergone surgery. So, when you awaken from your drug induced state following a surgery, my wife is the first person you typically see.

"Terrible" was her response to my question

about her day. When I asked why she informed me that she had her annual review that day. Apparently she is not a fan of the annual review. When I pressed her for the details of her horrible annual review experience, Susy acknowledged that she met all of the objectives required. So why was she upset? It seems that what bothered her was not the actual finding of the review, but the fact that her work was undergoing scrutiny. What made her nervous was someone else examining what she had done and declaring it "good" or "bad," "acceptable" or "unacceptable."

Apparently she is not alone. A November 2013 article on the *Business Week* website cites a 1997 national survey by the Society for Human Resource Management that found only 5 percent of employees were satisfied (42 percent were dissatisfied) with their companies' review process. The article goes on to say that even HR folks are not big fans of employee reviews, noting a 2010 Sibson Consulting study that found 58 percent of HR managers dislike their own review systems.[47]

A Review in Church?

So what about church life? When was the

last time you were asked to undergo a review of your service in the nursery? When was the last time your children's director called you in for a briefing on your teaching methods? Indeed, has anyone ever set an appointment with you to review your role as a greeter? Probably not. There are two big reasons why this is the case.

First and foremost, those of us who serve as pastors and ministry leaders are simply happy to have volunteers. At all. So, we tread carefully when it comes to discouraging a volunteer. The last thing we want to do is turn off a faithful servant by providing a negative review of their work. Most pastors highly value those people who faithfully serve the body of Christ by giving of their time, talents, and treasure.

A second reason we do not do many reviews of volunteers is simple: we do not know what to measure. Evaluating one's volunteer work in the life of the church can be tremendously difficult. And the more "spiritual" the work, the more difficult it is to review. If we are reviewing the lawn care team, that is not as difficult. Did the grass get cut or were there patches of weeds left standing? But evaluating a Sunday school teacher for 5th grade boys is a little more challenging. How can we determine what is being poured into those kids? Assessing one's success rate in spiritual matters is a challenge.

In addition to these reasons, faithful pastors are all too familiar with poor standards of evaluation. The two favorite measures of success in many churches is nickels and noses, or offering and attendance. If the offering and attendance numbers are good, the pastor is doing a good job. But pastors (and most church members) know that nickels and noses is not a good indicator of the church's health, vitality, or fidelity to the gospel. After all, there are many ungodly ways to boost both of those measures!

Thankfully, there is a way forward. There are other options for evaluating a person's effectiveness in a particular ministry beyond numbers. And such evaluation is necessary. After all, if what we are doing in the church is important, eternally-relevant work, making sure every member is serving as effectively as possible is an earnest undertaking. We cannot afford to ignore poor or ineffective service because we are afraid to lose a volunteer or uncertainty about the best way to measure his or her performance. It is better, dare I say essential, to know the truth about how a volunteer is doing in a given role. But before we get to the details of how to review the performance of volunteers, let's ask a prior question: is it biblical to perform a review?

Is Evaluation Biblical?

We want to be very careful not to approach the evaluation of ministry volunteers as if they were employees in *Fortune* 500 company. Indeed, because the church is the body and bride of Christ, we need to make sure that doing such evaluations has biblical warrant. While there are no direct texts that tell us to "do volunteer evaluations," there are passages that indicate that Old and New Testament servants were "evaluated." While I do not intend what follows to be a thorough examination of every instance in the Bible of evaluations being made of servants, a few should suffice to demonstrate the practice has biblical warrant.

In the last chapter we met three men in the Old Testament who were in charge of various areas of ministry in the Temple. We are told that Bezalel and Oholiab (Ex 35-36), as well as Kenaniah (1 Chron. 15:22,27; 26:29), had their roles for one primary reason: they were skillful at it. While it is not explicitly stated, common sense dictates that the way we determine someone is "skillful" at a given thing is to observe them engaged in the activity and "evaluate" how well they perform. So, there is in the very least, an implied evaluation of these three servants. The craftsmanship (and teaching ability) of Bezalel and Oholiab was observed to have been done well. Likewise, Kenaniah was skillful at leading the choir, which is why he had the job.

But, you may think, that was the Old Testament. Surely Jesus has a different perspective. Well, not really. Although it is not always wise to use parables to establish doctrine, the parable of the talents (Mt 25:14-30) and the parable of the tenants (Mt 21:33-44) do establish a principle that is applicable here. That principle is simply this: God expects fruit. In the parable of the talents, the one who did not use what he had been given in such a way as to earn more was reprimanded. That's a nice way of putting it. In reality, the one who bore no fruit, had his talent taken away and he was tossed outside (Mt 25:28-30). The point here is not that we should toss unproductive Bible study leaders out of the church, but that there was an assessment performed on how well each person did with what had been entrusted to them.

A similar observation can be made about the parable of the tenants. This parable has obvious messianic implications and it is not the intention to demean it by talking about evaluations. But it is instructive that the reason Jesus says the kingdom of God will be removed from those who reject the Messiah is so that the kingdom can be given to those "who will produce its fruit." The only aspect of this parable that is instructive for us is that God does, in fact, evaluate our effectiveness. He wants to know what we will do with what he has entrusted to us. One further point on this parable should be made. Because this parable is, in fact, about our receiving the kingdom of God as a result of Israel's unfruitfulness, it is imperative that we be concerned about fruit bearing.

The early disciples also seemed to believe in the importance of assessing a servant's suitability for ministry. Probably the most prominent occurrence is found in Acts 15:37-41. In that passage, Barnabas and Paul are planning a return trip to the churches they had established on their first missionary journey. Barnabas suggested they take John Mark with them. Paul was not a fan of the idea, to put it mildly. John Mark has apparently been traveling with the mission team and got homesick. In Acts 13:13 Luke kindly reports that he "left them to return to Jerusalem." Paul did not describe John Mark's departure so kindly. Paul said that he had "deserted them" during the trip.

Here is the key point for our purposes. Paul assessed John Mark's behavior on the first trip and found it wanting. He determined that John Mark was not ready to be entrusted with the demands of missionary life, based on his previous actions. Paul evaluated his behavior and found him lacking. It is worth noting, however, that Barnabas had a different perspective about John Mark. Whether his favorable opinion was due to John Mark being his cousin we don't know, but we do know Barnabas saw potential in him. Based on the fact that much later in his ministry Paul requests John Mark be sent to him because he would be "helpful to my ministry" (2 Tim 4:11), Barnabas may have been the one with greater insight. The point is that both Paul and Barnabas evaluated John Mark's performance on their missionary journey. The fact they disagreed is a reminder that such evaluation is an inexact science and should keep us humble and gracious as we engage in it.

Of course, John Mark is not the only person Paul evaluates in the New Testament. He commends Timothy to the church at Philippi as one who "takes a genuine interest" in their welfare. Indeed, his character was so outstanding that Paul said he had "no one else like him" (Phil 2:20). In Colossians 4 Paul is concluding his letter with a series of comments about those serving with him. He mentions that Ephaphras is a servant who is working hard; so hard that Paul says he is willing to "vouch" for him (Col 4:12-13). He also mentions Tychicus (Col 4:7). He describes him as a "faithful minister" who Paul is sending to them to encourage them. In the case of both Epaphras and Tychicus, the Apostle Paul has evaluated and assessed these servants and commended them to the church at Colossae.

There are other reasons for assessment beyond commendation. In 2 Timothy 4 Paul warns Timothy about several men who had done him harm. He mentioned Alexander the metalworker and urged Timothy to be on his guard against him. More important for our purposes, however, is

Paul's statement about Demas. We do not know what Alexander's relationship was to the faith, but Demas was one who had been a fellow servant with Paul. In fact, in Colossians 4:14, Demas is mentioned as being with Paul and Luke. But at some point Demas deserted Paul because he "loved the world" (2 Tim 4:7). Again, Paul is not neutral about Demas' behavior. He commends him when he is serving faithfully, and condemns him when he is unfaithful.

A final example from the New Testament shows another biblical reason for evaluation. In Colossians 4:17, Paul urges the church at Colossae (the recipients of the letter) to urge a servant named Archippus to "complete the work you have received in the Lord." This is a tremendous example of making a ministry evaluation and encouraging the one serving to keep going. While we cannot be dogmatic, it seems that Paul is giving a great word of encouragement to a man who may have been tempted to quit serving. Ministry has a way of beating us up and discouraging us, and it is possible that Archippus was experiencing the temptation to throw in the towel. Rather than quit, Paul urges him to continue serving.

360 Degree Assessment

Although we are not big fans of reality television, I will admit that my wife got me hooked on *What Not to Wear*. The show features Stacy London and Clinton Kelly, two fashion experts who try to help people learn to dress better. London and Kelly find all sorts of poorly dressed folks based on the recommendations of their friends. One of the first things the fashion experts do to help the bad dressers understand how bad they really look is to place them in front of what they call the "360 mirror." The hope is that the person will see what they look like from every possible angle and realize they need help.

The idea of seeing ourselves from every conceivable angle also applies to ministry and leadership. In 2005 John Maxwell wrote about how to develop into a 360 degree leader.[48] The big idea of that book is that a leader leads in many different directions, depending upon the relationship the leader has with others. For those under his or her responsibility, a leader leads "down." To those above him or her in the organization, a leader must lead "up." To those who are peers, the leader leads "across."

The flip side of Maxwell's concept is a 360-dgree evaluation. If, after all, we lead in those directions, it also makes sense that we can receive feedback about our leadership / ministry from those directions. After all, those serving in local church ministries have very similar relationships as those Maxwell describes for leaders. There are people who we serve "under" – our pastors or our ministry team leaders. There are those we serve "over" – those who we are actually ministering to or for whom we have leadership responsibility. There are those we serve "across" – those who are in the same role we are and who observe us serving. I think church leaders (and ministry servants) can use these ideas – plus one additional direction – in evaluating a volunteer's effectiveness.

First, consider the evaluation from "above." Church volunteers serve under the authority and leadership of their pastors and (possibly) direct ministry leaders, depending upon the size of the church. The smaller the church, the more likely a pastor will be the primary person "above" a volunteer. But as church size increases, the layers of ministry leaders increase. Regardless of whom the volunteer is serving directly under, that person plays a vital role in helping assess the effectiveness of the volunteer.

In my estimation, there are two key questions that a leader must answer for a volunteer. The first is whether the pastor(s) / ministry leader(s) believes the person has the skills, talents and passion to be serving in that particular area. Nothing is more critical than a word of affirmation that those in leadership see the skills, talents and passion in a person cohering with the area in which they serve. The second question is whether their pastor(s) / ministry leader(s) believes the one serving has made the ministry better by their service. Again, this kind of affirmation from leaders is vital.

It is also true that this type of evaluation is not always pleasant. It is easy to do when a person is clearly serving in an area that fits them and when they are making the ministry better by their service. The flip side is not as pleasant. It is essential, however, that those in church leadership as well as lay volunteers understand that a pastor / ministry leader's primary responsibility is the health and welfare of the body. Humility from leaders and a willingness of volunteers to submit to those in authority over them will make this a blessed process. Absence of either and it will be a disaster filled with hurt feelings and broken relationships.

The second direction that evaluation must come from is "below," that is, the people to whom the volunteer is ministering. For a Sunday School teacher, for example, that may be the people in the class. Just as universities ask students to review and evaluate a professor's work in the classroom, it is helpful to ask those in the class how they have benefitted from the service of the person under review. Feedback from those that a volunteer is serving can be a tremendous source of encouragement and refining.

A third direction for evaluation is "across." In mind here are those who serve alongside the volunteer under review. In a children's ministry setting, for example, this may be the people who are serving in the same (or similar) role. The key is to get feedback from people who regularly see the volunteer under review in action. It is vital to know if those who regularly observe a person serving in a given area believe that the person is cut out for that kind of ministry work.

A final direction for evaluation is one that Maxwell does not cover: internal. While ministry assessment from external sources of insight is important, it is equally important to assess what the Holy Spirit may be saying to the person serving. A series of questions that may be asked of the volunteer under review might include:

1. Do you have a sense of call from God to continue serving in this area?
2. What do you like best about where you are currently serving?
3. What do you like least about where you are currently serving?
4. How does serving in this area bring you joy?
5. How has serving in this area helped you to grow in Christ?
6. How would it affect you if you could not serve in this area?

These questions are designed to encourage the individual serving to reflect on the way God has been growing them through their service.

Assessing Effectiveness

It is my suggestion that the review process

as described above occur annually. Many churches have an annual time when they are filling ministry positions. I recommend the review take place approximately halfway through the service year. So, for example, in the church I currently serve recruiting new volunteers and establishing a service calendar occurs in August. In our situation, we would want evaluations of volunteers to occur between January and March. That gives the person serving opportunity to get acclimated to their ministry role and those serving with them enough time to form an opinion as to their effectiveness. More important, in my estimation, it gives time for a mid-course correction.

It is also important to reiterate that the goal is to evaluate effectiveness. We are asking the question: is the objective of the ministry role being fulfilled effectively by the volunteer under evaluation? We are not asking if they are the best we have ever seen at a given role. Nor are we solely evaluating their effectiveness based on attendance or growth in the ministry. Both of those are dangerous and unfair. Rather, at issue is whether or not the individual is fulfilling the task set before them in a way that brings joy to their life, spiritual fruit to the lives of those they are serving, and is validated by the observations of those spiritually responsible for them.

Having said all of that, we must humbly acknowledge the difficulty of making definitive (or final) statements about a person's effectiveness. Think back to John Mark. In Acts 15 Paul does not want him along because he deserted them in the past. But nearly 15 years later, he tells Timothy (2 Tim 4:11) that he needs John Mark.

Final Thoughts

Perhaps, like my wife, you are not a fan of an annual review. Maybe you are nervous about the idea that someone is evaluating your service for the Lord. Remember, the evaluation is not an assessment of your heart, your love for the Lord, or your character. It is intended to make sure you are, in fact, serving in your place of greatest joy. Indeed, we must remain humble both as we seek to evaluate those who are serving under us and as we are receive evaluation from those responsible for us. But we must not fail to evaluate effectiveness. Doing so will only perpetuate the frustration of serving without the joy God wants us to experience.

Regardless of whether you are a church leader or a Christ follower trying to determine your place of most joyful service, it is vital to evaluate effectiveness on a regular basis. If the examples above from the Old and New Testaments are accurate, God expects that we serve Him with skill and effectiveness. The role of evaluating effectiveness is to help make sure that we are hearing clearly from God about where He would have us serve. That is not to say that God does not stretch us out of our comfort zones or that doesn't occasionally surprise us with a ministry assignment. But it is does mean that God will equip you to faithfully (and effectively) carry out any and every ministry to which He has called you.

AFTERWORD

The goal of this book has been to motivate you to serve for the first time (and to equip pastors and church leaders to motivate you); to get out of the stands and onto the playing field of ministry. There is no other way to say it except this: a key to helping people discover their place of joyful service is to simply get them serving somewhere.

The question of how to help believers discover their place of joyful service to Christ began when my childhood pastor suggested everyone take a spiritual gift inventory. The conventional wisdom of the day seemed to be that, if only people knew their spiritual gift, they would begin to serve. Larry Gilbert was a leader in that movement, having authored several books and inventories designed to help believers learn their spiritual gift. But Gilbert has changed his perspective on the best way to engage individuals in ministry service.[49] In those early days Gilbert believed that if a person was taught about spiritual gifts and given an opportunity to discover his or her spiritual gift, that person would get involved in ministry. He has since come to believe that teaching on spiritual gifts and spiritual gift discovery will help those already serving to be more involved and more efficient in their service, but is not effective at motivating people to serve for the first time.

Please do not wait until you figure out the perfect place to serve, but be faithful to serve with the gifts you have in the place God has you. Do something. Serve somewhere. Take a risk. Be willing to give your skills, talents, and passions away for the sake of God's kingdom. If you do, you will discover a joy unlike any other.

NOTES

[1]Information on the Just Do It! ad campaign from the article about "Nike, Inc" and "Just Do It!" on Wikipedia and from http://nikeinc.com/pages/history-heritage.v

[2]C. Peter Wagner, *Leading Your Church to Grow* (Ventura, CA: Regal, 1984), 131.

[3]Thom Rainer, *The Book of Church Growth* (Nashville, TN: B&H, 1998), 113.

[4]Robert Pochek, "Toward an Ecclesiocentric Model of Spiritual Gift Identification" (Ph.D. diss, The Southern Baptist Theological Seminary, 2011); available for download at http://digital.library.sbts.edu/handle/10392/3738

[5]Kenneth Berding, *What Are the Spiritual Gifts?* (Grand Rapids: Kregel, 2006), 201.

[6]Henry Blackaby and Mel Blackaby, *What's So Spiritual about Your Gifts?* (Colorado Springs, CO: Multnomah, 2004), 52.

[7]Ken Hemphill, *You Are Gifted*, (Nashville: B& H, 2009), 193. To Hemphill's point, the cover of the SGI-Gilbert states: "Discover your spiritual gifts in only 20 minutes!" See Larry Gilbert, *Spiritual Gift Inventory,* rev. ed., (Elkton, MD: Church Growth Institute, 2005).

[8]The idea that spiritual gifts are controversial is a reference to the debate over cessationism/non-cessationism, the number of spiritual gifts indicated in the Scripture, etc.

[9]The Myers & Briggs Foundation, "Original Research" [on-line]; accessed 14 February, 2011; available from http://www.myersbriggs.org/my-mbti-personality-type/mbti-basics/original-research.asp; Internet.

[10]The year 1972 is cited by Wagner, *Your Church Can Grow*, 71, where Wagner states, "I believe the real turning point [on the matter of spiritual gifts] to be the publication of *Body Life*, written by Pastor Ray Stedman of Peninsula Bible Church in Palo Alto, California. The unusual popularity of that book in 1972 is due largely to the receptive climate for spiritual gifts that had already been five years in the making."

[11]C. Peter Wagner, *Leading Your Church to Grow* (Ventura, CA: Regal, 1984), 131.

[12]Rainer, *Book of Church Growth*, 113.

[13]C. Peter Wagner, *Your Church Can Grow* (Ventura, CA: Regal, 1976), 74.

[14]C. Peter Wagner, *Discover Your Spiritual Gifts*, updated and expanded ed. (Ventura, CA: Regal, 2005), 74.

[15]Ibid., 20.

[16]Leslie B. Flynn, *19 Gifts of the Spirit* (Wheaton, IL: Victor Books, 1978), 21.

[17]Bruce Bugbee, Don Cousins, and Bill Hybels, *Network: Leader's Guide* (Grand Rapids: Zondervan, 1994), 78.

[18]The following is a sample of the books and materials concerning spiritual gifts and their use within the church that utilizes a similar definition of spiritual gifts: Wagner, *Your Spiritual Gifts Can Help Your Church Grow*; idem, *Discover Your Spiritual Gifts*; Bruce Bugbee, Don Cousins and Bill Hybels, *Network: Participant's Guide* (Grand Rapids: Zondervan, 1994); Dan Reiland, *Spiritual Gifts* (Atlanta: Injoy, 1998); Ray C. Stedman, *Body Life* (Ventura, CA: Regal Books, 1972); Greg Ogden, *The New Reformation* (Grand Rapids: Zondervan, 1990); Rick Warren, *The Purpose Driven Church* (Grand Rapids: Zondervan, 1995); Craig Keener, *Gift and Giver: the Holy Spirit for Today* (Grand Rapids: Baker, 2001).

[19]Wagner, *Discover Your Spiritual Gifts*, 22-23; idem, *Your Spiritual Gifts Can Help Your Church Grow*, 42-44; Fortune and Fortune, 15; Gilbert, *How to Find Meaning and Fulfillment*, 33-36; Bruce Bugbee, Don Cousins, and Bill Hybels, *Network: Participant's Guide* (Grand Rapids: Zondervan, 1994), 25.

[20]Hemphill, *You Are Gifted*, 34-35.

[21]Hemphill, *You Are Gifted*, 31.

[22]Berding, *What Are the Spiritual Gifts?*, 77.

[23]Carson, *Showing the Spirit* (Grand Rapids: Baker, 1987), 34.

[24] Kenneth Berding, *What Are the Spiritual Gifts?*, 79-80.

[25]Ibid., 80-82.

[26]Kenneth S. Hemphill, *Spiritual Gifts: Empowering the New Testament Church* (Nashville: Broadman, 1988), 181, and idem, *You Are Gifted: Your Spiritual Gifts and the Kingdom of God*, 160.

[27]Hemphill, *You Are Gifted*, 160.

[28]Ibid.

[29]Carson, *Showing the Spirit*, 17.

[30]Thomas R. Schreiner, *Romans*, Baker Exegetical Commentary on the New Testament, vol. 6 (Grand Rapids: Baker, 1998), 19. According to Schreiner, the resolution of ethnic disunity between the Jews and the Gentiles has now become the majority position among New Testament commentators regarding the purpose for the writing of Romans. For a list of commentators taking this position see Schreiner, *Romans*, 19 n. 42.

[31]Ibid., 650.

[32]Hemphill, *You Are Gifted*, 120.

[33]For examples of the various explanations for the writing of Ephesians, see Andrew T. Lincoln, *Ephesians*, Word Biblical Commentary vol. 42 (Dallas: Word Books, 1990), lxxi. John MacArthur, *Ephesians*, in *The MacArthur New Testament Commentary* (Chicago: Moody, 1986), vii. William Hendriksen, *Exposition of Ephesians* (Grand Rapids: Baker, 1967), 61. Ernest Best, *Ephesians*, The International Critical Commentary (Edinburgh: T & T Clark, 1998), 75.

[34]Rudolf Schnackenburg, *The Epistle to the Ephesians,* trans. Helen Haron (Edinburgh: T & T Clark, 1991), 34

[35]Harold W. Hoehner, *Ephesians* (Grand Rapids: Baker Academic, 2002), 102.

[36]Hemphill, *You Are Gifted*, 160.

[37]Ibid.

[38]The exception to this may be the list in Eph 4:11. However, the position taken here is that the gifts mentioned in that passage describe individuals within the church that are, in themselves, gifts to the body.

[39]Berding, *What Are the Spiritual Gifts?,* 82-83.

[40]C. Peter Wagner, telephone interview by author, 5 April 2011.

[41]Hemphill, *You Are Gifted,* 133.

[42]Clowney, *The* Church (Downers Grove: IVP, 1995), 66.

[43]Wagner, *Your Spiritual Gifts Can Help Your Church Grow*, 81-83.

[44]I am thinking here of the gifts described as miracles, healing, apostle, prophet, tongues, interpretation of tongues, word of wisdom and word of knowledge in particular. Though not wanting to engage in the cessation debate in this work, I acknowledge that these gifts are clearly unique to Christ followers, though I would maintain they have been replaced by the completed Scripture.

[45]Hemphill, *You Are Gifted*, 185.

[46]Ibid., 185-86.

[47] http://www.businessweek.com/articles/2013-11-07/the-annual-performance-review-worthless-corporate-ritual

[48]John Maxwell, *The 360-degree Leader* (Nashville: Thomas Nelson, 2005).

[49]Larry Gilbert, telephone interview with author, 9 March 2011.

Made in the USA
Charleston, SC
11 February 2015